Ruins of Index
and Other Places

POEMS BY

LEE MICHAEL ALTMAN

ARTWORK BY

LEE MICHAEL ALTMAN

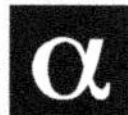

ISBN 978-0-9989931-0-2

Contents

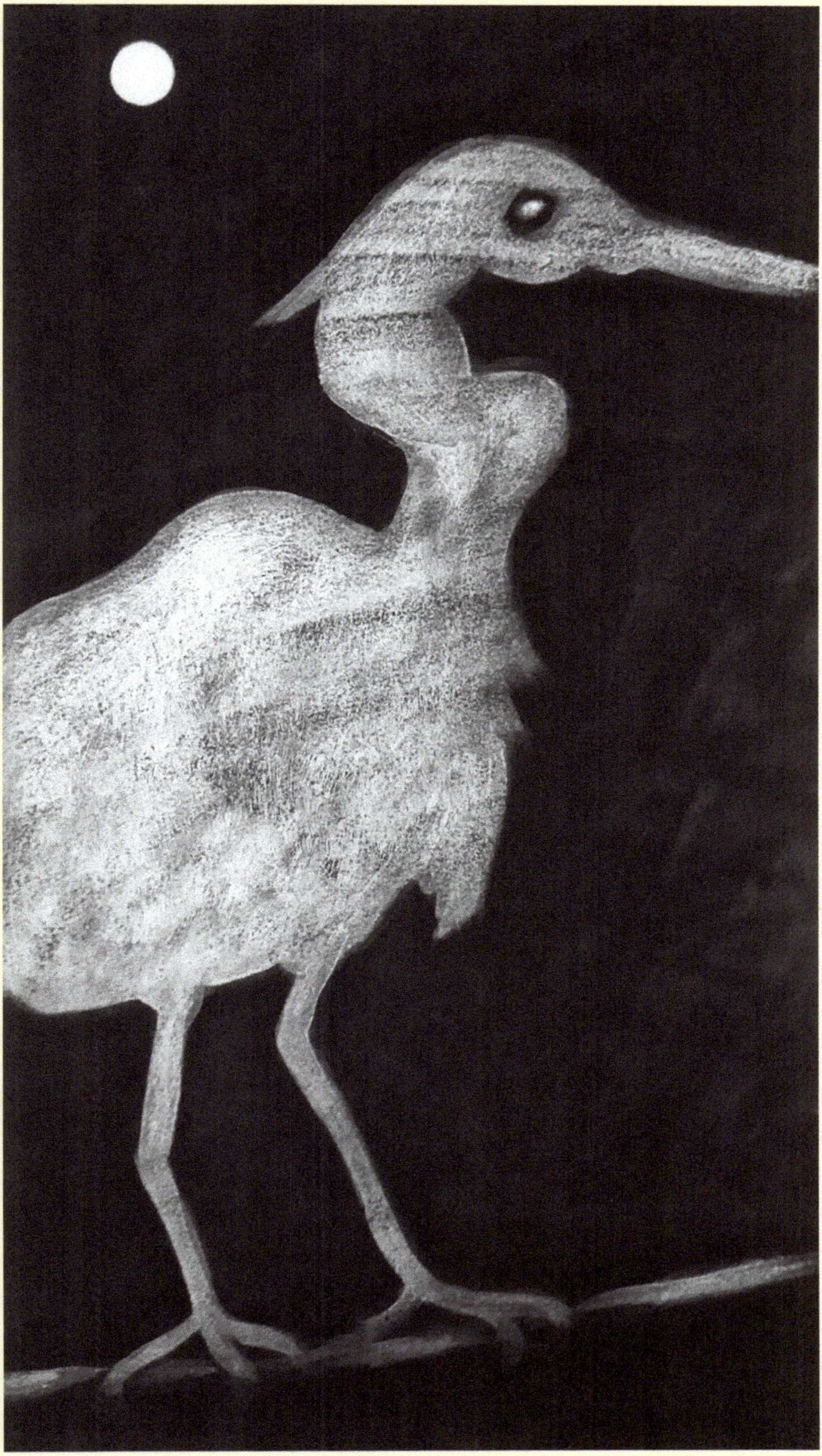

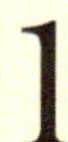

1

Ruins of Index

North Fork 1962

Named for a finger pointing
to heaven, now
it's just a granite quarry

on the Skykomish River.
In 1898, the town was
crowded with prospectors,

drifters, grafters.
The Great Northern RR went up
to Monte Cristo, over to Spokane

then from Stevens Pass joined
the West to Eastern tracks.
We camped in a tunnel of firs, fished

for steelhead in pools
of the Sultan Stream.
Summer stretched above two

long rusted wires,
hand over hand to the other side.
A trail along pine planks took

us into the woods, over
narrow-gauge tracks,
to a clearing of cabins.

That was where she rose from the red
brick chimney — I mean Annabel,
the ghost of the Summit

Hotel, its gingerbread
fallen into its own gutters,
its white smoke curled into fir tops,

wraith of an errant
death. Knock, knock.
Out stepped an old miner —

Annabel's white fingers
flamed from his ears, billowed
out his mouth,

She's not home. Go away.

She is not home.
When word came down from Silver Mine
that her beau died in

an explosion, she hung herself,
although he was alive and rushed to find her.
Years later he could not live

with her memory
and shot himself.
Now she hungers above Sunset

Falls, climbers can feel it
and fall to their
death in the wide Skykomish.

Buildings burned,
she leveled all she had
promised to keep.

Meanwhile copper ate through the town,
then wood
for miles around.

Now just the granite cliff of her hunger
in the mist,
her icy breath.

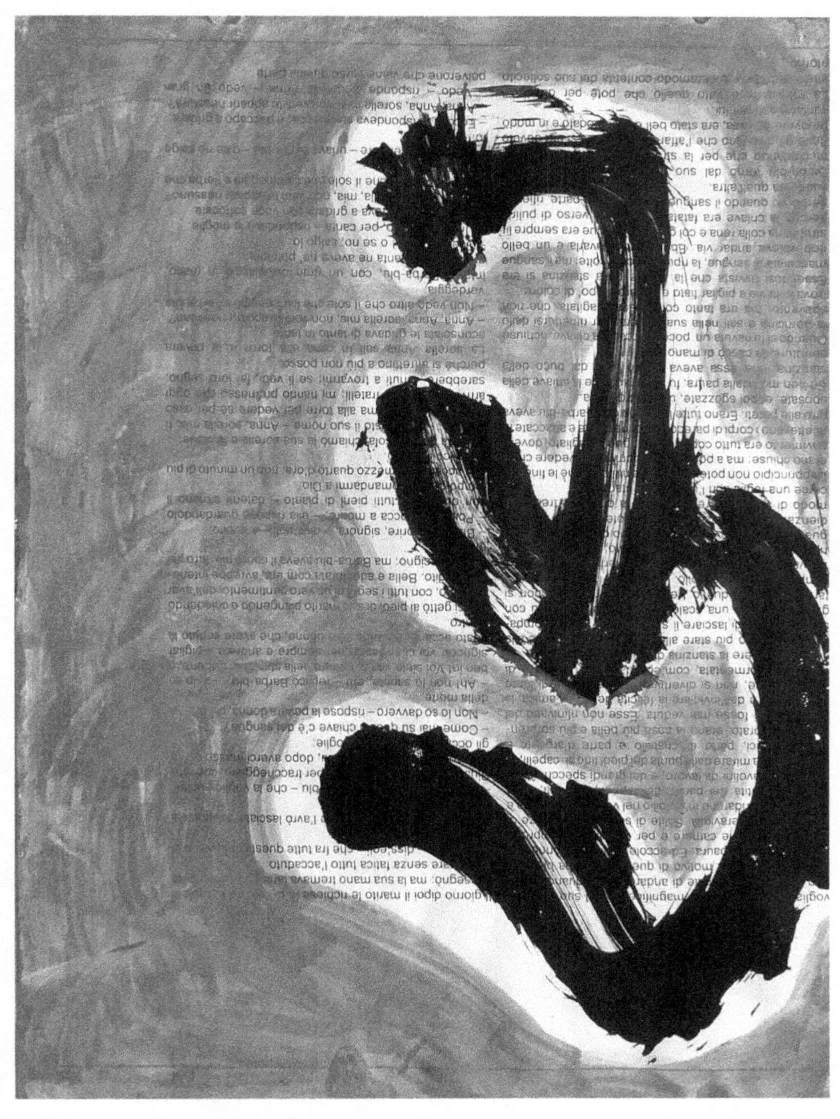

Seattle Burlesque

It had died many times,
when as teenagers we snuck into
the old Rivoli Theatre,
up a fire escape though balcony doors
hidden in a back alley.

We peered down on the red stage,
into the wings, sagging flesh held by
operation zippers, dyed red hair, white powder,
a drum set banged it out below the stage to bumps,

her grinds, the cymbals clashing as she threw
out her hips, the sequined g-strings sewn
from scraps, blue smoke rising around her
up to the balcony we coughed in, until the manager

caught us, then we were in the basement bawled at —
the whisky bottle in the haunt of mirrors,
thrown out of NY Delaware & Cincinnati because of film,
television, broken dreams, collapsed veins,

secretive lost house-wives, abortions gone awry,
hiding out on First Street — he was balding, potbellied
chewing on a dead cigar stub, spit-drooling over a
chin stubble, in the corner half-a-bag of groceries,

the orange suspenders, the pee smell, his baggy pants,
behind him a father/son act waiting to go on,
another dancer arriving from the outside —
had I actually seen Blaze Starr or Tempest Storm?

Eat your hearts out guys — Hey boys, do you want to
scratch the candles back for a quarter? Hopper paintings
of strippers in NY, Carol Doda in North Beach, Miss Indigo Blue
in Seattle — we ran down the streets, all the way home.

Uncle Lester's Laundry Route

He had to watch me, a six-year-old, in the back
with the new drop-offs and the old pick-ups,
staring out the truck window as he careened
the hills of downtown Bellingham —
laundry made a beast of him

drove him to drink and smoke,
keep yr head down, I'm a lightn' fart!
through the smell of steam and starch,
the bundled sheets and tablecloths,
the napkins — the moment

he tossed the bags in, I piled them on
my circular fort, as the truck pointed west,
downhill, Lester spitting *Just stay here
til I'm done!* ran into the barber shop
with a load, a shot of whiskey in the can,

out again running, smoking
at the wheel, as my window spread its smoothness
over the white laundry — I'm holding on, with
Uncle Lester crazed in the mirror, drooping-lean
off to Mrs. Eddicott's Boarding on 44th —

I'm waiting for lunch, a coke at Woolworths, not this
rolling forward, in a metal box with bags,
the shape of light in the door beside me, the infinite blue
an index of everything, bound into something else —
you've been a good kid t'day – gave me no grief Lester said.

Longview Plywood, 1965

Beginning in the Green Chain, sorting the sweet sap skins
peeled from timber, I pushed the wet sheets into kilns.
Kevin drew hearts and letters on them, already lost signs
before they burned off in the heat, he liked

to slam his fist into his hand, mutter women's names,
sometimes not writing, carving the letters, one of a
band of loners from the Bataan Death March, walking skeletons,
they met every year in Longview to drink and twitch.

Rifle-butt beating, starvation shootings
tropical heat be-heading, throat-cutting
sub-human animals, luminescent glass shards
lifting off in the Philippines.

There was Gordon who drove the Forked Lightning at
breakneck speed without honking around corners,
his crazed eyes in the folds
of the maggot blankets at the Death Camp.

There was Carl the ruddy-faced Foreman
who threatened a pink slip
each time he saw me working —
divorced, loose-cannon, brother Jimmy hanged.

I stayed at the Green Gables, a rundown Room
& Board with a 24 hour kitchen for lumber men,
forestry majors from Penn State, young Kerouacs
between States, retired Choker Setters injured from

flying chain accidents unleashed from logs.
There was Jackson who sat on the porch and drank, catching
a cat by the tail and hurling it into the yard, or Russ the kitchen chef
who drank Old Grand Dad in a water glass near the stove.

There was Sam who never came out of his room day or night,
then died silently his stink preceding him. Their nightmares
screamed down the hallways muffled by the rattle
of fans, there to scatter the Pulp Mill

stench which ran all week for years on end.
A Plugger and Sander I punched out odd pieces
with a swinging pneumatic arm
and plugged them with oval wood patches, the forklift

brought in banded bundles, I unloaded them one sheet
at a time, belt-sanded, and graded them AB, AC, AD
or recycled rotten ones into the *Hog* waste
chopper men lost their hands to. Moving

among jobs in the Plywood labor pool
during the graveyard shift, I spent a week
on the Columbia pulling logs into a water saw,
sorting sizes with long hooked poles, jumping

from log to wet log in the dark,
and in the first rays of clear light, the Gillnetter
Trawlers started out to sea, stirring
up the seagulls down the river, until I trudged back

to Green Gables and slept all day
in a small room with dry moths along
the window sill, clothes unwashed, empty
beer bottles, letters unsent. Then

on the last day I took the Greyhound
back to Seattle and slept my first real
sleep, watching myself in the window
wondering if I'd ever return.

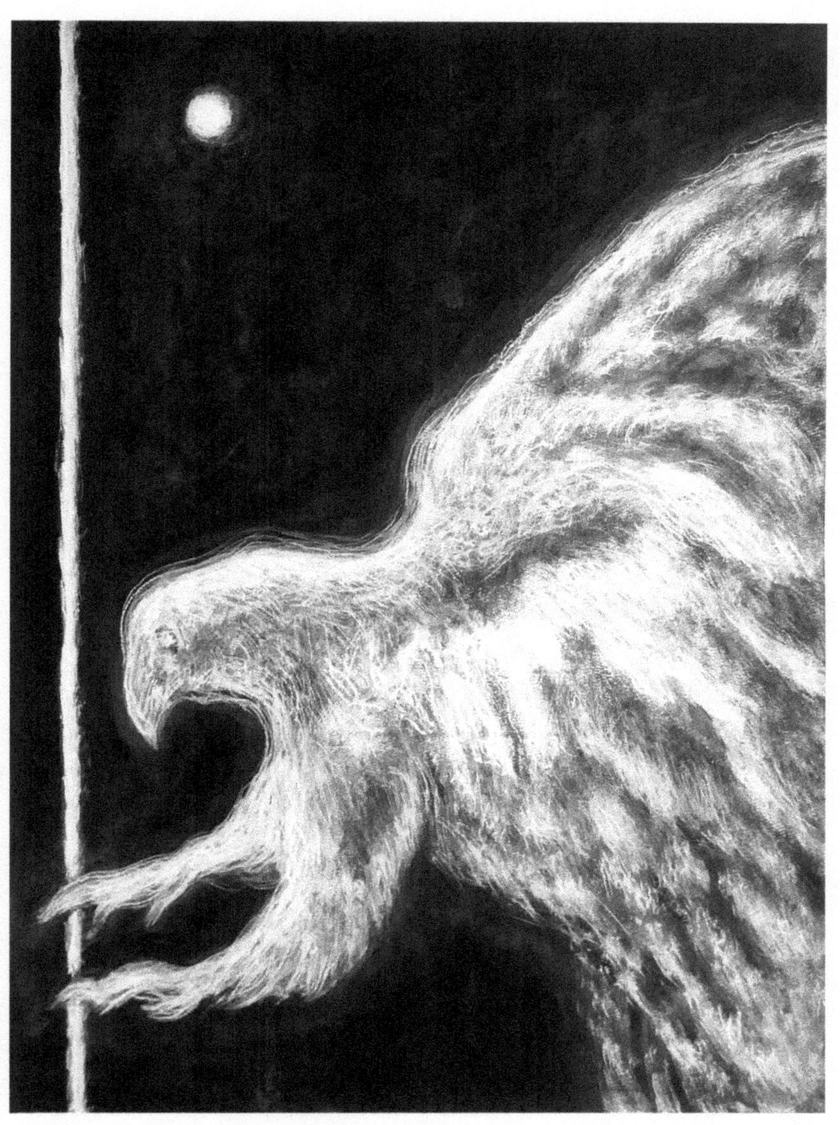

Bellingham, 1950

I was five when taken from my twin brother
to live with an aunt while my mother had a divorce,
the small house barely contained my
two teenage female cousins and aunt — I slept on the porch
covered with window screens in Northwest winters.

On a propped up bed
I found myself on the floor with the dog, muddy boots
and pruning equipment for the backyard apple orchard.
My cousins studied HS anatomy in books and on myself,
labeling in lipstick my body parts or putting up my hair

In curlers with the latest styles, a test to see if
they liked them first. At the beach their boyfriends hid my
clothes or tied me round a spinning log at the lake. Laughter was
the common twist of the day. I left for long silent walks in the woods
and found solace in

Foxglove, hyacinth, brown toadstools along the creeks filled
with rotting leaves. At night I heard owls screech and branches crack,
the moon's ghostly shadow over footsteps up the gravel walkway,
back from the dance — their tousled hair and wet taffeta from pawing in
back seats of grey Pontiacs.

One night the orchards burned, an orange glow woke me.
I closed my eyes and let the colors bleed down
the pathways I knew away from house and into the woods. Spiraling voices
brought me back to screaming, red lights whirling, the fire brigade arriving,
I ran under the porch wrapped in webs, among dusty apple crates.

In morning I walked past the woods, past homes,
farms and other orchards, often I was lost, turned around
from circling, from spinning arms outstretched, from an empty center.
Until in moments of sky and cloud my eyes
squinted hard orange sparks against deep black space.

I entered translucent floating water, flowing
into eddies and out again, long ribbons unraveled, carried
me down streams past old storm-piled branches, past discarded
toys left in decay, brackish pools laden with cardboard,
and out to sea.

Pioneer Square

The first studio I rented from Broderick
for $12 a month the realtor never billed, we never paid —
three years went by

until on our way to Mexico, we sent the keys back
from San Diego
with an excuse of having left Seattle years earlier.

Those days everything was sure, immediate, we
were poor and young without questioning, and put gestures
down the way

our nerves vibrated, then went on
to something else —
even the other thing was a Calling, like walking into

another room to change one's clothes, we danced
with it, to the studio around the Square, the
wrought iron pergola

cut across benches of forgotten men with
bottles in paper bags,
fluttering pigeons fed on popcorn while the bronze statue

of Chief Seattle watched sourly — when someone
had a pint of whiskey, homeless
hobos knew and descended on it for sips.

Before climbing the long stairs past the red brick front,
the entry way a polished path in the dust hard from rain,
a pile of letters to long distant tenants: Joan Miracle, Herb Buster,

Merle Marty, notes left still tacked on the walls: *Meet me
at French Laundry 1:30 — Pay me for the Paints or else! —
Joz, I was here and went to Portland.*

The cold wind of early mornings, thin and sharp from Alaska
our shepherd's coats barely kept out, bronchitis, the stocking caps
we trudged around in — some inner resolve

kept us going, we held little sunlight and brought
sack lunches to the studio on Pioneer Square —
it was a long narrow room on the second story built

after a devastating fire, windows covered by black netting
at the end facing the alley, the floor vibrated, echoed
down the halls above a tavern from a weekly rock band.

A marble sculptor lived and worked in one studio whose
white dust filtered throughout the building, I painted on rolls
of drawer liners in spray paint and oils, houses crumbling down,

winking cats, and Kandinsky take-offs. I smeared auto body
putty with my hands
onto abandoned doors, found lumber left in the side streets

along skid row, mixed paints until they cracked and fell apart.
One year Moroccan smugglers encamped in tents
they fashioned from blankets and rugs,

hid out from the law or generally incommunicado,
later the poet John Logan lived there, wrote about Seattle
houseboats and mallard ducks, haunted the bars of First Street,

alleys of the bums.
The second studio a block south off Pioneer Square
I shared with a painter/theatre director from New York

in a large Gothic window ballroom once a flophouse —
in the back rooms old paintings left, cannibalized by traveling artists,
one room a forgotten capsule of the 1880s in dusty grime:

furniture, calendars, clothes, mirrors of down fall,
here was a sense of fatality which lingered on —
we surprised ourselves with painting bright new images,

the process of our growth found in the long walks downtown
past the Farmers Market, pawn shops, loggers, grocers —
the traffic of the Viaduct freeway hurling past the piers

without notice toward suburbs and forests — we took it all in,
I painted blue faces in oil on cardboard, backgrounds
in glossy stop sign enamel. Upstairs Bill Ivey painted

large abstract canvases, on off-days played a lonely flute
echoing into the ballroom we mixed into our paints —
along his studio window sill, a rusted tin can end started a series

of circular white paintings, *something Tobey showed me* —
GI art school grant in SF with Rothko & Still — once a paratrooper shot
in the guts, he held them from falling out, walked miles, a real tough guy —

the WW II back story of US Abstraction, until he left the darkness behind.
Joseph and Erika lived in the ballroom balcony loft,
a rambling one room we braved the cold with whiskey-laced coffee.

Joe's work ranged from Picasso to Ivey and back again, he pushed the paint
around in a workman's matter-of-factness and somehow put up with my early
starts — if we didn't enter by a narrow grease-blackened entry up the stairs,

we exited by another into the knife-stabbing alley off First Street —
on the roof of liquid-hardened tar and seagull shit we went to
sun on a summer day, then walk down to Pier 54, Ivar's Acres of

Clams or Ye Olde Curiosity Shoppe with shrunken heads from Ecuador,
Sylvester the mummy from Arizona, Indian masks, Siamese twin calves.
The creosote pilings slapped with Ferry Boat oil and NW winter rain.

We knew we were on to something and went back to the studios
on Pioneer Square.

The Young Oldman

High School theatre make-up
bought at Max Factor on Capitol Hill,
taking the trolley downtown,
wandering through the Farmers Market
as Oldman, white beard with baggy clothes.

Hi there Gran Dad! grocers shouted —
feeling older, limping into the part
smelling the fresh salmon and greens
through my spirit gum fake beard,
stooping down to walk the gauntlet of First Ave.

Fresh, bigger than life,
the real bums fading into storefronts, skulking
weary on the long pavement
from rain, from drink, from no money —
immigrants wandering on a thread.

Cascade miners, shopkeepers from Omaha,
loggers from Longview, orchard pickers
from Wenatchee, watching as I passed
until on the railroad tracks south
of Pioneer Square ...

Two women from Frisco
had hopped the Coast Freight up
to Seattle looking for a flophouse
or some action —
in my face.

They saw my false beard
called me *Cop-get out!*
ran down the tracks
yelling, cursing, laughing.
I'm standing alone, no longer an Oldman —

The names loom ahead
rutted paths taken
unawares, by solace or cunning
mixed under NW sullen skies,
the smell of damp leaves.

The garbage rot in alleys
the empty winds off the Sound,
my youth looking toward old age —
left blank without knowing.

Following Mrs Cutts

I haunted her store on University Ave,
the *Puss n' Books,* owned by Mrs Cutts
cluttered with twenty cats, asleep in the windows or atop shelves,
cat piss and old book dust and Scarlatti.

She was a balding square shape in a sack dress stained with food
reading as she shuffled with her scaly elephant legs
down the Avenue, no teeth, hairs on her chin,
heels of her shoes broken down like slippers.

I traded books for a Leonardo tome,
she tapped her bony finger on it, saying slyly *Temples of the Abstract*
or for a selection from her button hoard each
she said appeared in the pages of Proust, James, or Dickens.

Once I saw her on the bus to Lake City
I followed her home to a sunken
bungalow overgrown with vines,
stacked inside were books destined for the shop.

Once I knew she lived just blocks
from me I roamed around the place
evenings mornings afternoons,
her husband shouted in the dark, a dog barked.

Mysterious prizes, unknown rare books from thrift stores
or discarded in bins around Seattle,
the books she carried home had meaning and weight,
they were hidden and read before selling.

Histories biographies ledgers of domain,
green poetries and chimera pioneers
of unspoken memories filed in dust
below the Farmers Market and First Avenue.

Someone found her dead on the toilet
in the back room of the shop,
her cats asleep at her feet,
a book in her lap.

Racetrack Sandwiches

Maybe the set of meat-carving tools
on loan, the Greyhound that carried me south

to Long Acres, the flow-swarm of magnetic
starlings writhing against the orange sky,

I knew I had to do something about my life,
hunched over the smell of lost books.

I stared past the neighborhoods, stared into
our amnesia, saw our lives as obstacles

in the path of the obvious. I had my long
knives and forks, my chef's hat —

I was ready to carve. But what was I
to care about? What had I known?

When I had time I walked into the stands
and saw the black binoculars' lenses

glinting red, the floors strewn with torn
tickets, the grifters and losers lurching their way

home. Speakers boomed the horses' names
over the screams for more: More loss!

more grief! More sandwiches! Prime
rib on sourdough, eight bucks. I carved

and thought the pink centers oozed like horses'
muscles, driving the hard hooves,

gripping the curve, groaning,
jockeys' sopping backs hanging on a bet.

Boxing Lessons

It was summer in Seattle
what little there was,
when my father took me downtown
to the Joey Velez School.

A warehouse with a boxing ring
in postwar grimy shadows,
Joey's withered leg took him on
a career fighting his stricken riddle.

The locker room silk trunks too large,
my skinny chest bewildered, lugging
heavy gloves stinking of unwashed feet
from body blows —

Past punching bags or jumping rope:
Fathers yelling *Get your gloves up*
Step up into the ring
Throw a Right jab Right cross

Make friends with Pain —
Goya's men on knees beating
each other with clubs — our monsters
against their monsters, Nietzsche said.

B/W 16mm boxing films
neighborhood men gathered to watch
& cheer famous fights, ex-G.I.s smoking
out of the looming hunger for air.

Father blown up in Pacific Theatre
spent years in an Aussie hospital,
lost his manly pride & returned to US
a DC salesman drinking on lost roads.

We touch gloves toe to toe,
When the bell rings Hit him hard.
He died of kidney failure, rare tumors
only 5 people had, written up in textbooks.

The Island

It was my uncle George, an ichthyologist,
taught marine sciences at Bellingham,
lived on a hill above the Bay, built boats,
carved Indian birds, and took us at low tide

down the zigzag cliff-trail past Red Cedar
and Spruce to the dock.
He rowed out every day circling the island,
Osprey and Eagle

roosted in Douglas Fir, small narrow trails
wove throughout the island,
dark pockets
of creature stirred as we passed.

Chuckanut Island weathered sandstone
changing with tides,
we re-moored our skiff often before
foraging in a forest of Madrone

their slick red skins peeling in summer.
A midden of broken oyster shells
where the Salish met to feast
and left a white mountain of shell-loam.

Along the shore we dug razor clams,
heaved their wet-heart shapes in a gunny sack
and lugged them across the island
to a Northeaster Dory painted black & white.

*

Charlie from Crete joined the Bogart family
up the coast, out of San Francisco and
Belgium — they picked me up in Seattle,
a kayak strapped to their roof.

We headed into the strait on a cabin cruiser
for Rock Cod and Salmon to make Cioppino
stew, later we pulled up pots
from the dock and tossed the Crabs in too.

In full summer air, salt heavy in our lungs
we steamed into the San Juans,
heading south to small coves,
Coho Salmon sheltered in deep waters.

We plowed through and over the language
of days, cut up vowels and kelp in the oily wake,
unsnarling silence for the first moment,
sailor's knots, tenacity of handshakes out

of poor shame, all green words
drowned in the sea's dictionary. Charlie
and Stan threaded the lines, brass reels
rolling blue filament, hard-life hands

straight out of the Depression, delivering
furniture flights up for pennies,
loading frozen steers out
of East Bay warehouses.

*

Then the Silver Smelt hooked over the side,
fish guts thrown
to the Dog Sharks, frenzied
up from the freezing depths — what was it

that wavered in heat? what divided
itself beneath us?
What conjured absence in sea salt,
or reeled in the razor fin Rock Cod

that we beat thrashing on the floor,
their white skins turning coral
pink, then blood mauve
in quiver and gasp?

In the end, we forgot the hunt, headed
back to Chuckanut Island, milky
white fish eyes passionless peering
out of a plastic red bucket.

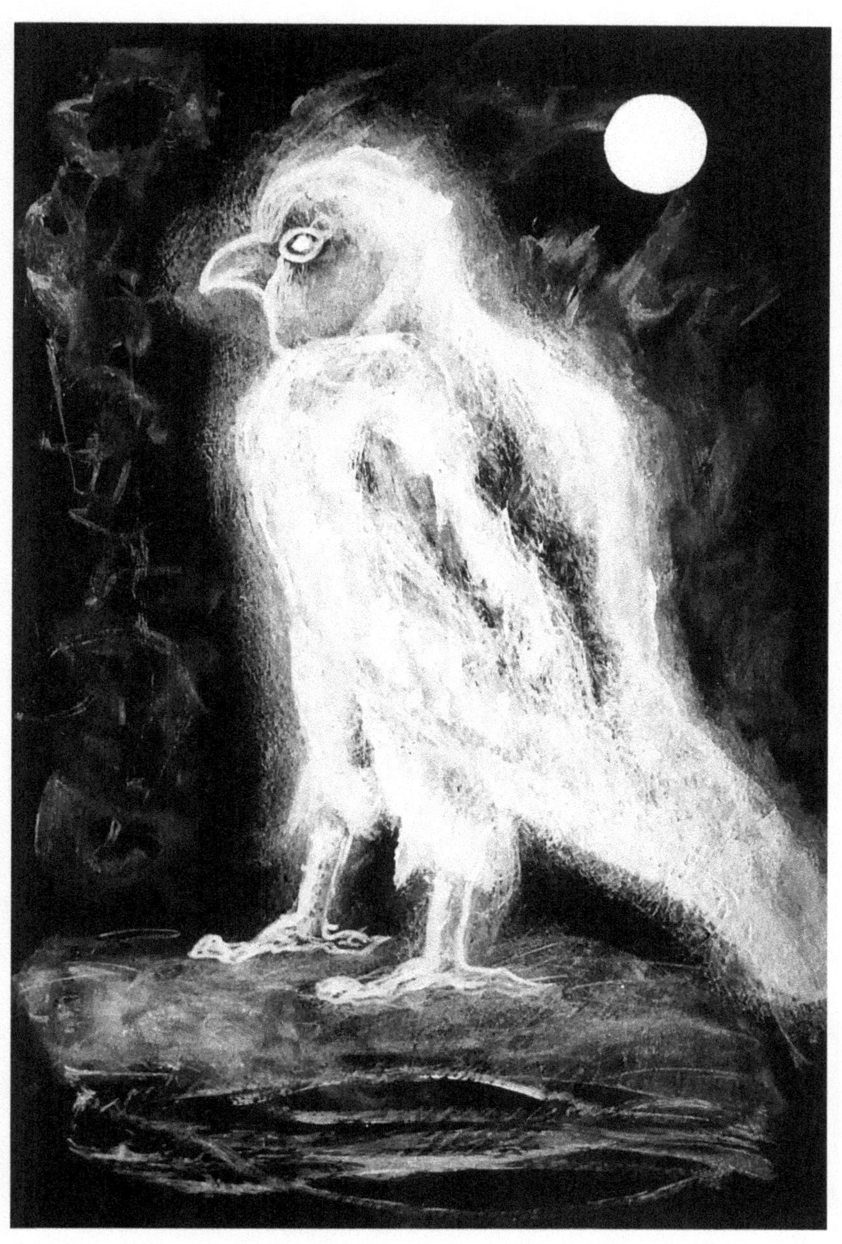

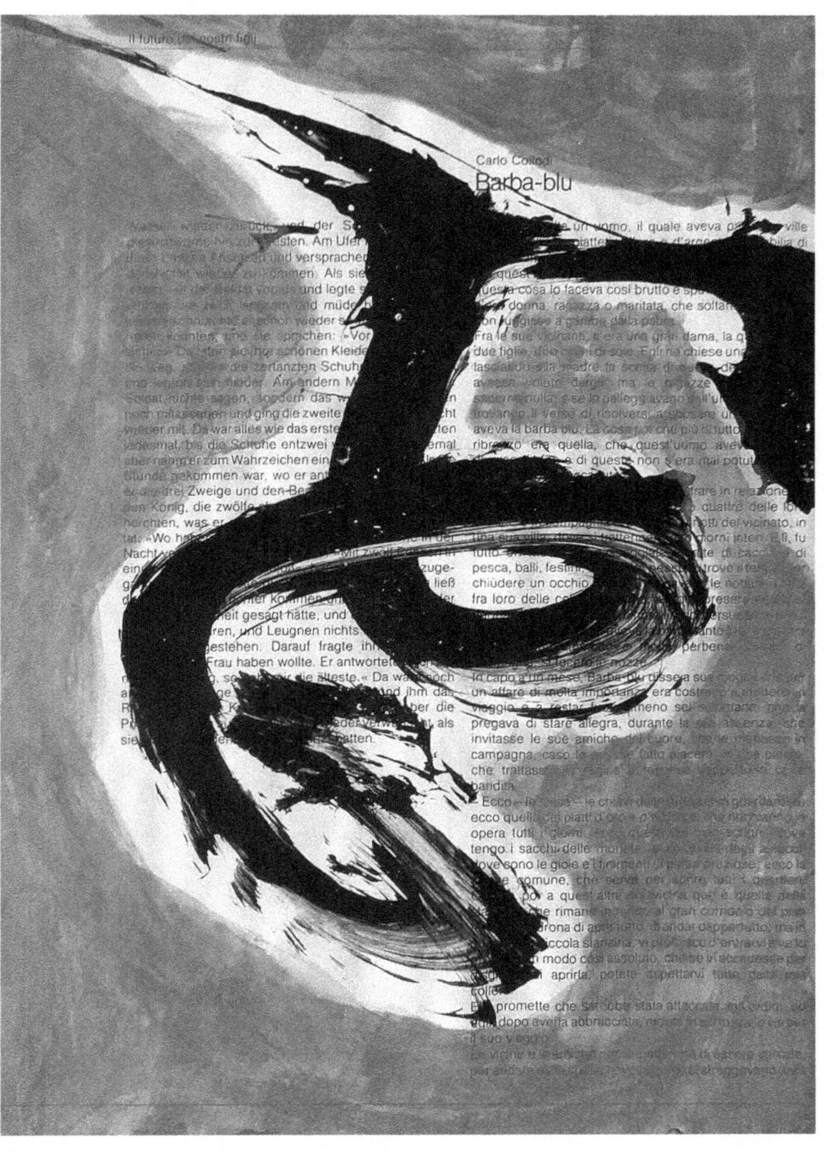
il futuro dei nostri figli
Carlo Collodi
Barba-blu

Magnolia Beach House, 1952

the savagery of the match

My father picked me up from Bellingham
and took me to his new wife and home
in Seattle, a summer cottage on Magnolia Bluff,
without insulation we braved the NW winters.

A movable platform hanging from a concrete
bulwark cranked down to the sea at low tide,
the expanse of beach reached out flat
to starfish, rocks, seagulls diving and dining.

I carried the Stockholm Syndrome there into sunsets,
identified with my Bellingham tormentors yet
longed to escape the Magnolia ones — lit stolen matches
in the shelter of a hollow log, against the wind.

What was there to laugh on the beach, the salt blooms
left glistening around the blue-scarred pools,
the white seasons stuck in quicksand,
my running steps turning over and out to sea.

Ferndale

Ferndale was originally
called Jam from a log-jam
on the Nooksack River

Ferndale front yard
— a ring of toad stools ghost-like
in moonlight

*

Ferndale cherry tree
— spitting seeds on the root cellar roof
through curled tongues

*

Ferndale hayloft
— black panther & leopard
played in a cave of hay blocks

*

Ferndale bedroom wall-
paper stained from the downpour
— apocalyptic landscapes
we watched for hours

*

Ferndale covered causeway
— echoes of footsteps
in a long tunnel to the woodshed

Ferndale skeet shoot —
a duck blind covering a dugout pit
of spent shot gun shells

*

Ferndale clothesline
— two bloody fox tails
drying in the evening wind

*

Ferndale attic bedroom of my uncles
— beds unmade, rifles on the walls
the black plastic crow calls

*

Ferndale used engine oil aroma
— opening the implement shed
a sailboat under construction

*

Ferndale shore at the Strait of Georgia
— a long walk on a warm day
bringing hot dogs and cool pop

*

Ferndale donkeys Rosie & Baldy
soft muzzles and wiry fur —
my uncles took to Fire Lookouts for the summer

*

Ferndale grain shed of harvests
— forbidden entry year round
only to happy farm mice

Ferndale rusted water troughs
of green mossy bottoms —
collected rainwater
for years and years

*

Ferndale butchered black cattle
taken from the holding pen
yelping their last
— one at a time

*

Ferndale cows hung upside down
skinned length-wise
— then chopped into cutlets
and frozen for the winter

*

Ferndale general store
started by grandfather
who carried depression era families'
rent for years — nothing else to do

*

Ferndale log cabin added on —
built around and over many years
until a grandson and family
lived in a mansion

Ferndale log cabin later
taken apart and put in a museum
— after the aluminum company
poisoned the farm land for decades

*

Ferndale farmers at the courthouse
protesting metal contamination
disappeared — too vocal
against the organization

*

Ferndale farm remains
a clump of trees
— shackled together at the top
of a desolate hill

*

Ferndale original fence
cobbled together at the road
— in memory of what started there
and never lasted

Ferndale Farm, Washington State, 1879-1952

Pirate Monkey

Was kept in a large bedroom cage
two of my childhood friends
fed for their pirate father, who played
the role in a Seattle summer SeaFair parade.

Sprung from edge to edge screeching
the shit the piss piled on newspapers,
banana peels & oranges uneaten
scattered into corners.

Two brothers knew their monkey
only when strangers entered the room,
and took him on their small shoulders
as a kind of practice for the father.

Still he is double-fake coy, smiling
in his temporary body, yelling out of the
parallel universe, we only know our reasons —
a whispered double helix: nothing has changed.

Oceanic outlaw, fiery buccaneer, squalid
stealer, the raw rudder of flotsam, burning
galleons dreaming of white dawns,
the flags of nations to plunder.

The Solution

I put them to sleep in a mason jar
of carbon tetrachloride, then
mounted them pinned onto cotton,
where they flew out of sea fog:
moths, crickets, beetles, giant wasps.

Lined-up in a cigar box, or soaking
stamps for fading watermarks,
crowns of Austria, daggers of Ethiopia,
the lodestones of eye teeth — magnetic
microbes in sea turtles.

Frigate birds migrated
by verdicts wrapped in
envelopes, weighing down balance,
our feet in our final fetal curls,
in white muteness, mucus on the

Backs of stamps, the first and last result,
the light across walls the insects slept on,
before I took them in their moment,
the whites of my eyes
already turning over, back in the box.

Liquor Store Chronicle, Seattle

Who got me that job for Christmas stocking shelves
at the state liquor store on Capitol Hill?

What a crowd that year buying booze and getting
ready for the New Year, I stroked the shelves

with long handled feather dusters and pushed bottles
forward, cut open new boxes and stocked

them, looking out at the many hands grabbing
and clutching out into the cold night street.

*

The universe knows what time it is
time to create the law of large numbers

Inventory counting constant
bases of 5, 10, 25 multiplied beyond

Quick math on a box top
mat knife pie cuts on cardboard dust ribs

Circumference & vector points
on a clipboard, about bottles, pallets of bottles

Warehouse boxes brought in by truck
& forklifted into long blocks we opened to stock.

*

Fingers stained by blue counting ink
of the cashiers:

Barney lived in a trailer with his son,
a stoned rocker who drove a red Trans-Am
without hubcaps, dropped Barney off to work.

Big Mary in a floral Hawaiian Mumu
waddled to the cash register from the back
employee lunchroom, chewing gum
and blowing pink bubbles with a collapsed snap.

Nervous Cliff in khaki clothes,
pencil-thin mustache smirking
with quick outbursts of high laughter.

Roy, store manager, deaf to the music
of the spheres, the Muzak piped
through the store, because of the clinking bottles
we stock clerks in the back pushed forward, toward him —
sullen, bitter after childhood polio
left him limping from the hip,
dragging his bad leg to one side.

Mei Ling, practically a shadow, withdrawn as if
in wooden masks, her receipts without overages — left
on the bus exactly everyday 6:30 sharp.

Reki, district guy, always had a smutty joke,
had been with the State Liquor Board
for decades and knew the connecting ropes —
when I was up for review and reinstatement
I took the written test and passed,

the only loose end remained downtown.
Reki gave me a bottle of Red Label whiskey
wrapped in four bags I took up a high-rise building
to a State politician (who often hung around
the liquor store near election time canvassing votes)

— he took the bottle smiling promising
nothing and it came to nothing later.

*

Why is the sun going blind?
something large, inscrutable
emerged from the clinking bottles
& the deaf manager.

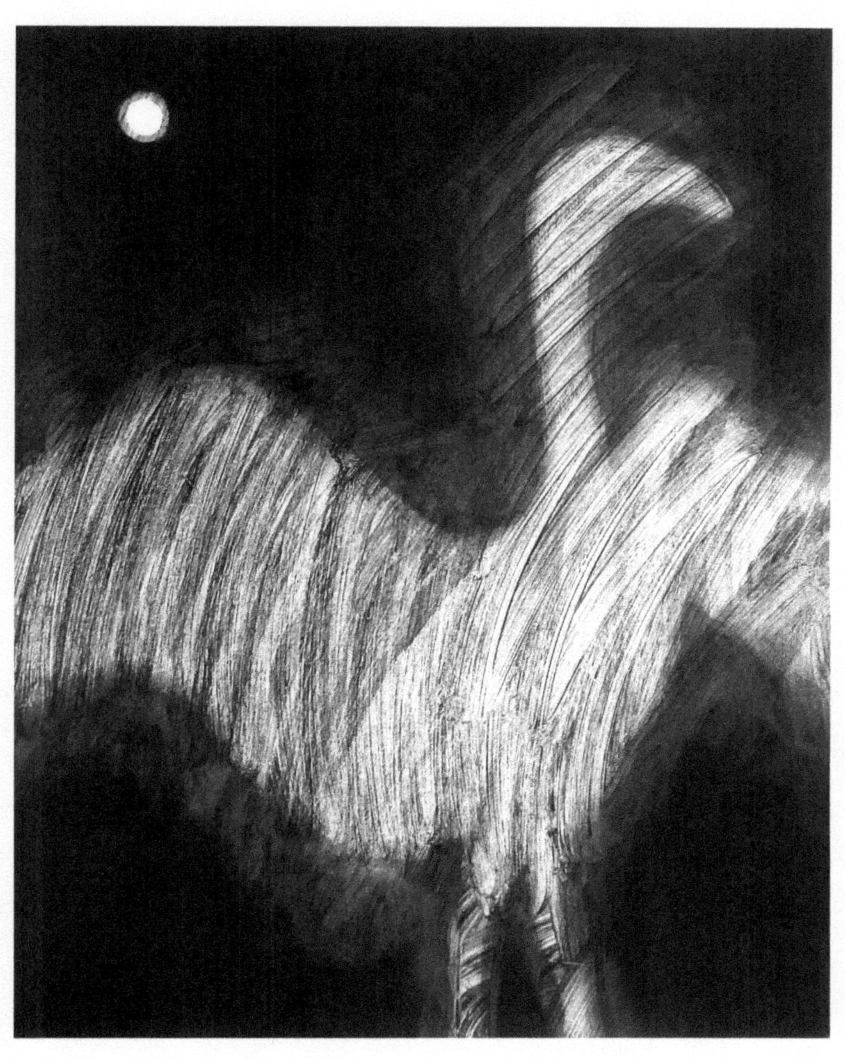

Box Factory, Seattle

What straying molten form
torso legs or arms might fit
within a box for bullets and guns,
remain unanswered.

Could we spoon out body broth
hunched into the mess,
slurping with mournful glee
the abrasive concussions

Over purple eyelids
leaking at edges putrefying
the knotty pine slats,
hissing shouts & embraces too late?

The sleeping terror
nailed harder now,
if the gun jammed in single
shots aiming at the wall

On automatic released a spray
of steel points —
Rat tat rat tat tat tat
what we never forgot.

Gary drafted into Nam,
convinced he could make a difference
without guns
went into tunnel caves of the Cong

To talk them out,
shot him up & lost his balls
and never recovered —
then sold candles at the Farmers Market.

The son of a banker
once played Satie on piano,
lost his lovely wife
the keys to a kingdom

Stored in a box.

Watching Caryl

When I first met her I was a dishwasher
at a restaurant in downtown Seattle,
I had just returned from Santa Fe and was living
hand-to-mouth on Capitol Hill with old friends.

She was a ballet dancer from the Tri-Cities
where her father had bought her a blue Mustang
leather hardtop. We both were out of place at the
restaurant and knew it, waiting on the business crowd.

Caryl stood out as a waitress with her long dark hair,
long legs and a round Italian face. We looked at each other
and knew in spite of our jobs we would be together soon,
it was Fall and the leaves were ochre-colored. I took her

home to the big house on Capitol Hill during a theatre party.
She undressed in the dark room and slipped-in with me
cool and soft, our sweet-tipped juices pooled in our thighs,
our eyes squeezed out white phosphenes, our moans burrowed

into the room during the party downstairs, an orange shaft of light
across the floor reflected on our bodies, we came together.
Years passed: Botany and Art at the University, vacations, camping
trips, long walks, dinners, parties together until our eyes fed

each other in the deepest waters. One day her old boyfriend
Rodney came back from Vietnam, and it was over.
She went back to him like a cheap novel and I started watching
them, I couldn't help it. They lived happily without seeing me

as I watched them in hallways as they kissed. I studied their
timetables, with her apartment key in my hand I'd go in when
they weren't there, to move things around, then I took back my
gifts of drawings and paintings, until one day I thought they

had left for work, with the key I opened the door and found
Caryl staring at me, she screamed and threw things.
My shadow-stalking self, unredeemed, not possessed —
I returned the key and never watched them again.

Those moments of waiting cleared my dark body,
a sick dread drifted through me then, I saw myself from above
in the secret spaces I waited in, floating clear, no longer there,
my feet fatally set in the shoes I wore those days.

Crash at Snake River

We came to in the front seat of her Chevy,
the railroad tracks stopped us from tipping into the river,
we climbed to the dirt road and collapsed, our bodies
curled into fetal shapes and slept.

Named Penny Nail by her humorless father,
a car mechanic, who sent her to college in the wheat fields
of southeastern Washington state, with a Chevy Classic
totaled by myself over a cliff at the Snake River, her

dark brown hair, brown eyes, dark nipples —
the graduating senior hot for a freshman, myself a beginning
force only too willing to leave my eyes troubled in slipping
waters, the skin peeled by silky magenta, by last cries.

First time at the back of an apartment during a party
on University Ave, a curtain separating us as we
squirmed over coats and scarves, her dark eyes pouring
snake water into mine, until we fell asleep.

On Vashon Island we hiked from her parents' cabin
to the upper meadows and made love in the wind,
my tongue on her iron blood, her gasps, my
yelling into the night, then woozy love talk,

as the tides lapped in the wheat hills
of Palouse, our blue shadows moved across
the snowy fields, or spring at Snake River
fused between giant glacier boulders.

The river's endless looping, startled her eyes
her yes at the center of unexpected twisting, in
morning light on water after a storm, her currents
among the cattails in eddies of Snake River.

The river more ocean than earth
winding through eastern prairies, the wet spasm
of her opening out, the evening glow
above the milky spiral arm.

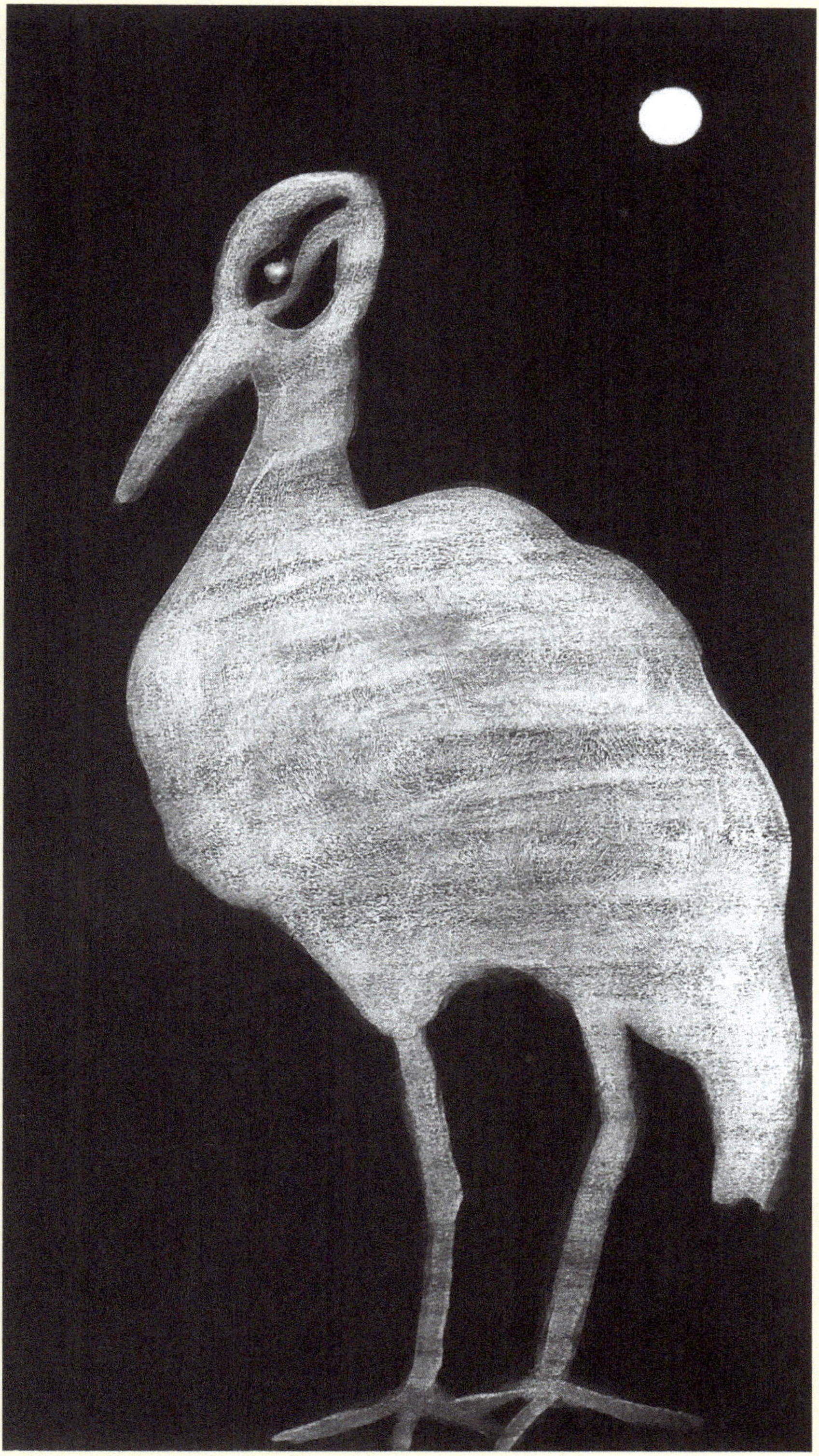

2

Dream at Fidalgo

For Morris Graves

A dark wing passed over your cabin,
the moonlit-tide-lapped circles —
startled your dream: white heron
perched on the chalice by the door.

Your coat was ink and night loam — out of it
sprang the white light of the San Juan Islands,
rupture from the city, the tops of mushrooms
and blurred feathers dropped in hurried flight.

Priestly black languid sleep of exile and return,
behind galaxies the mourning dark,
lunar snakes rising, swaying into winter,
voiceless thresholds of your long walking nights.

You built walls from crates and found lumber along the shore,
carried through the woods and dragged upon the rock,
hammered into sanctuary near wet leaves,
the bird sounds in thickets all the mornings.

Oil lamps lined a wall near your painting table:
mulberry parchment, tempera, thin celadon bowls with water,
paper splattered from use became new fields
for bird-men in few essential strokes, eyes added later.

    Pitch black veils, inky washes laid out
    charcoal combustion firing the white trapezoids,
    rock whipped brushes, waves, fir branches,
    the corpses of men turning into white lines.

February cast long shadows of you dancing nude
in the woods, toilet paper trailing from your butt,
whooping with the owls, clapping sticks against tree trunks.
In blue ink, you painted the perfect circle in one fading stroke.

    Some nights, black kelp entwined your bloody feet,
    the mallards' green necks glowed
    under *the milky stories of the moon,* you wept
    paintings and envied the sea, carried a minnow in your beak.

You ate what you grew near the fir-bordered meadow
and what you bought in Anacortes — rice, barley, tobacco, sockeye
salmon — what you found in the night woods fed you most,
it feeds us now, white ciphers from the dark of Fidalgo.

White Writing

For Mark Tobey

Riding the #31 into Pioneer Square mid-winter
to my painting studio among the soup kitchens
of Skid Row, I saw you hunkered down in three coats,
a black beret, your calligraphic beard white

>as your inner writing that lights the North, writing ice
>bridges in long arcs across the rivers.
>I stared into you over ribbons of the white field,
>magnetic flow behind appearance, you stared back

uncomfortably resigned to public transportation,
caring only for the lunch you were about to eat —
White, first source, salt, zero of form,
blinding time in a seed, the brush and ink and paper.

>Held hard in the twilight corona, now enfolding
>the rain-cast suburbs all the way to decrepit
>First Avenue. Your paintings electric fields
>wrapped in butcher paper, carried home.

You got off at Bon Marche, I followed you
to the Farmers Market, haunt of bums and grocers,
white dissolving stalls of produce and fish,
like language you signed with your long brush

processed from no name, from the trajectory of flies,
from nothing, the movable vortex.
At the Athenian Cafe
you met Graves for a beer and sandwich —

Graves ordered dark wings and white ink.
You had just white ink.
I had a grilled crab sandwich and a Bass ale.
You said to the air with a flourish: *The immediate*

    and open pure movement ...
    Graves replied deftly and black-
    eyed: *no, the dark wing*
    in moonlight ... I wanted to say
    green fire-eye and force-line, while out

the window gulls spiraled over the chugging
ferries, beyond them the Olympic range in snow still
hoarding the light of February, Puget Sound —
black sea water hungering for silence. I settled

    in a corner of the dark wood and watched
    myself watching you from the back: white hair,
    snug beret, hands held up gesturing blind calligraphy on
    the waiting paper of the clouds.

Frog Pond

For Theodore Roethke

A silver garter turns its eye in silence
toward me, larvae heaving under green,
the bubble-domes of frogs torn loose from pods
and wiggling free, into the swim, the burst

wide aureole of the sun. The scotch broom billows
pollen on the water, a shroud floating across
the sky's reflection weeps pure yellow.

I jump the stream over gnarled fennel
the badger had seized when the moon
hid at midnight — I kneel before the first
forest interiors of rocks stained
by violet algae, the circling sky still slept

in the summer morning rustle of bird.
I turn my voice inside out, renewed fire
protected in morning's dewy leaves & snails,
my body catches early light.

I open a path through pine
boughs, the birds' whistle
mingling the piracy of dawn by hissing
bees, southern winds rigged with vapors

of moth spores & fallen seeds
fall on my feet singed from trembling
names and night ashes,
scarlet-orange plants unfurling the horizon, vales
of sudden fumes fall down the sap trees.

I place my life beside my clothes, the light
changes my words burns the thickets —
can I return to what I was — my hand encircles a new sweep
of all that a shadow could contain, the trees raining
their needles from fury to ash until

the sun is up and carries me on
blindly into the white noon, two mourning doves
settle into an open spot, the insects
sleep in shadow and forest tendril
surround me suddenly in place.

Mandelstam in Brittany

it was as if the stone thirsted
after another existence

We drove from beach to inn to beach
again, then stopped that day to
see the Carnac stones, martyred upright in
late afternoon, standing figures cut

with solar circles, aligned to the stars
in chartreuse lichen, of silver fur
spreading up their sea-backs,
derelicts with bound hands.

His wife had scattered autumn apples down
the strolling paths, we stepped over them
out of eerie deafness, down the Moscow streets
the Atlantic rose to his waist out of the Gulags,

as he awaited the firing squad, heart attack
of the tyrant century — the stones oozed words:
I'm not the wolf of my blood, but a child
opening to the sun as we drove on.

The Mole

This process of burrowing, leaving the
surface untouched, gnaws at him,
the deeper he goes, the more unpredictable —
troops skewering those in their way,
lost sonatas drizzled into rock walls.

The refugees descending the ladder,
into the skin bag of ten thousand things,
his pale mole eyes intent on one thing,
digging for nothing-known, what drew
him on, an affirmation of matter itself.

He lived by robbery with violence, at
daybreak, the hour to vanish into streets,
a stray dog sniffing along walls, rose-hidden
branches twisting into trees,
a soft shadow, resigned to birdsong.

Bishop's Travail

She went on naming places, living among the multicolored
labels, shields of orange palms mapped on turquoise triangles

enameled, scarred by handling, illegible
red tangle of the sea's words, ghost spores, demented

chorus, spread across the floor in Boston.
Her luggage shook with pollen, witness

to moon-lined trees in Brazil
the sleeper feared at equinox.

Circling from Nova Scotia to Key West to Rio —
the sole author a scar in her scalp, a bridge

of lightning, she went on naming, all
the echoes against an edge of memory wholly

her own — the morning star
a single point across 2000 distances,

filigree ruins sewn into embossed purple
mountains, two rivers, a continent hidden

in terrible oxygen, in a slant of light, she wrote
whenever southern breezes took her away.

The Lamp

On the desk near the door Grand'mere's silk shade,
tattered yellow from all seasons the door
opened or closed, like a heartbeat, or the heat
thunder that followed me from Boston to DC
the summer she died.

Now a circle reflected in
a bulge of turquoise gold-speckled ceramic
I see my hands in. The desk an oak expanse that
white papers line at the edges, a range of winter
mountains turning to wings, to long exchanges.

Further on, surrounding it, sea fossils found at Año Nuevo,
shell spirals in rock, black obsidian, petrified whale bone,
Chiton wing spines — and between these two poles
like a glass of water by Stevens, circles Grand'mere
centered in lamp light and tatters, reading the pages.

Citizen & Scientist

every private citizen has
public responsibility

The scientist said
walking along the Potomac —
after I had asked, had insisted
he tell me, *are the oceans dying?*
and after a long pause, many steps
with head bowed, finally —
we have only 20 years left of life
as we know it … it's irreversible.

He fell back and walked alone
without talking again.

Sound waves from
the magnetic field, blue origin
of our first scream —
one word formed around the tongue,
the eyes rolled back, red sparks
against the black background —
figure eight currents trembling along
the blue sphere.

What can technicians learn
from a poet? the small increments of
scientists' study, the long evaluations
without a final report submitted,
as years pass and then
the methodical data presented to
a committee is bound into a book,
put on a shelf for further analysis — if the
Lobbyists don't kill it before it reaches the public.

Our paltry lives swamped by special
interests, by short-term greed
beyond the tipping point, a roasting pan
left in the fire — the end cycle, or can this
blue sphere heal itself without us — enraged
by pretenses, the direct insults going on
around us — what's in the box?
I can't say what I'm really thinking
until I've beggared the departed, the fresh water —
everything green soon will be brown.

Grand'mere Maxine

Was the first white woman
born on an Indian Reservation in the West,
her family the Spences owned
a general store & traded goods for beaded belts
once or twice a year, made little otherwise.

Handed down a single-shot Winchester:
Indian good luck sign carved
on its wooden stock, for the bagging
of prairie dog steaks and soup — the land
yielded ruby garnets in a block-long dish of light.

Pine trees outside of Colville, threaded
by stellar jays, Fibonacci cones, Canadian
winds, tribes of the given earth — submerged
her eyes in painting, the ochre-sienna
of nudes bathing along the Colombia River.

The winds swept the south hills of
Spokane, a red tile Mediterranean
along an extinct volcano ridge —
the pulsed-glances teaching painting
& ceramics at Holy Names, a studio at home.

Measuring the once dazzled messengers —
she read me the African Queen, the movie
with Bogey & Hep singing down the Ulanga
to Zambezi — Maxine lounging in morning negligees
swept along by the overflow of choruses.

We spent the summers painting white chords,
spinning bowls on the wheel, my solace
climbing black lava hills or watching her garden
the cycles of terraces — the lavender that bees
seized ungraspable in ordinary sentences.

*

She was already frail in
the early stages of chemo, hair sparse
mostly bed-ridden, when she rose
her robe dragged along slippers for bird portions in
the kitchen white-bright mornings of Maine.

*

At Three AM, I cut off her nightgown
to wipe up what she had lost
control of — her tears all night from the shame
of dying, then on Maui, I waded out into the water
shadow beyond shadow, a green flash on the horizon.

Dust of clay, coal & pipe smoke riddled her
artist's heart, her lungs, those gnarled hands
which shaped a life, a seeing that formed a language
in paintings, sublime spillage of the dialogues
in circular necessity — I thought she might be

Wind gliding in the hidden branches along
the blue arc of autumn, color traces
startled by the source of night — a thin transparency
passed before the moon, the sound of scattering
leaves made the window drop, a struggle of breath.

*

In the Cascara grove of slender trees
I took all their bark for money, a gunny sack full,
one long cut and two short cuts, their skins
came off in long rolled parchments, leaving
wet ivory figures in dark woods — were they screaming?

I walked farther back to forests, what collects
round the edges, birds rhyming in pine trees,
I scraped pitch for months into milk cartons, a dozen
or more lit on fire, floating lanterns on Lake Cavanaugh
one night only at the end of summer.

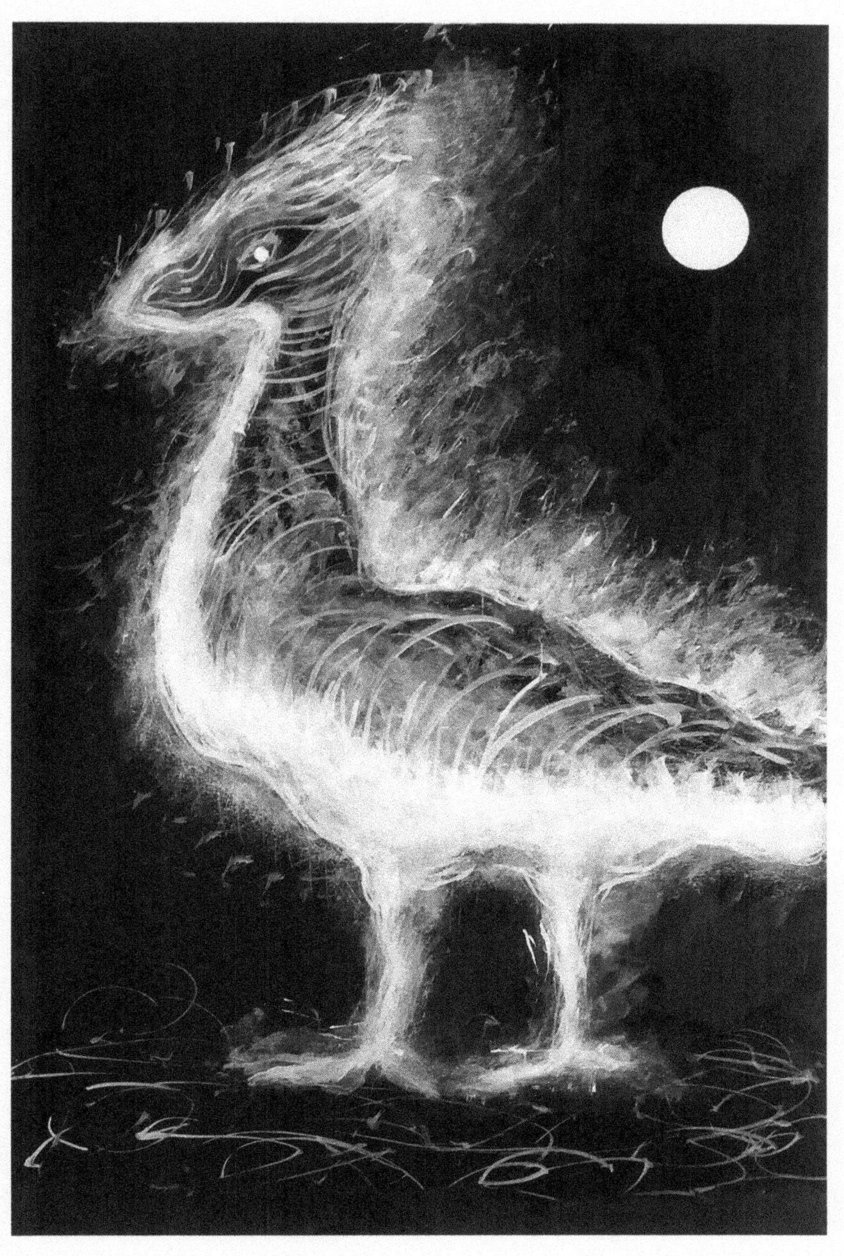

Spinoza

A dreaming striped tabby
tiptoed through the hour
curling around our ankles without socks
at breakfast, sleeping on laps after lunch —

shooed-out as dinner finished, lingering in
dark-meowing to return at the door, gathering
transparent shadows of violet evening
in the backyard, moon-bathing Raccoons

basking on lawn chairs, their little hands clasped
behind striped necks, their white eyes
radiant through masks — were your friends
or the Osprey clutching a saltwater perch

in its talons, its steely eye & chiseled beak,
its dignified pose surveying the water —
a cat for the sea in Chesapeake Bay.
Small sparrows clamping in mornings,

two fluttering spiral-ribbons up & over
shear-spinning their extreme affection
for your whiskered mad eyes, curiously lit up.
Animal friends know heaving waves of deep trance

and hold them,
the cat curls into its alpha kinship, imparting
circular minutes of color sound —
the unfinished utterly entwined, purring

nothing is yet known
everything answers resoundingly
to everything else — this cat cavorts with
a neighbor's white cat, what just is …

as an absolute necessity, the fur
of a self-caused perpetual system, a little heart
bonding to other forms, called Spinoza.

Night Hookers, 1980

Leaving Paris, Jacques driving a Peugeot 340 with Bach tapes
took me to the airport for a night flight, a taxi to the hotel
Washington Mayfair at 5 Curzon Street, central London
with continental breakfast and Elvis Costello on the morning telly.

Off to the National Gallery on foot, brownstones and dreary-sooted
streets reaching to Piccadilly Circus: pigeons, stolen-ware-hawkers,
old vaudeville performers.
Inside, the Turner paintings, early skies bloodstains

from his father's barber floor,
late white fields all brushstrokes waiting to be glazed with fingers
and a rag.
Rembrandt's extreme contrast of Hendrickje bathing in a river,

lifting luscious oil paint drapery
exposing the dark triangle, her legs wading into the night pool.
The sublimated apples of Cézanne, yellow-green-orange-russet

made in short strokes,
early abductions, rapes, murders, the black clock without hands,
the crimson shell —
later his landscape geometry constructed in planes of small

sensations, heroic, classic.
The balding bearded recluse of Aix, the brick red earth round
Mont Sainte-Victoire.
Back out to Piccadilly Square, afternoon crowds milling about

the Eros statue,
winged archer on one foot, a performer near the fountain, his pants
rolled up, tap dancing
to his own records, doing a female impersonation with an orange wig.

Freshened up at the hotel, then dinner at Tiddy Dols in a cave
under Shepherd Market, later walking
through Mayfair Park, the night hookers beckon winking
in cars under hazy street lights.

After several passes round the park, I talk to two pale women
in a red Fiat and ask how much?
Rembrandt's last self-portrait as *Zeuxis* — grinning mouth half open,
eyebrows raised, bankrupt

with all his worldly attachments gone, the freely-applied golden
impasto, vigorous in wet paint.
Turner's *Departure of the Fleet* — his last act having sailed into
carved-out light, filled with flickering daubs

with brush-knife-fingers, the final rally coherent,
breathing into the limitless sea.

The Recycler

Morandi knew bottles, painted them
all his life, centered him as now placed
before us, the chromatic greys of shapes
in daily familiarity, even in friendliness.

In unhemmed pants, two shirts
and broken shoes, he drags the flow
of daily bottles, his stubbornness
glimmering beneath the grime.

If our lives are in constant
becoming, these endless
bottles brought to him
for weighing and placing into

barrels stinking of saliva, piss, stale beer —
blur beyond knowing ourselves, except
by repetition or frayed will, his memories
turning over and over again.

On island beaches he ran as a child,
slightly smiling now in his beaten-down
thank you sir and passes a store slip
for money, his eyes humble-weary-resolved.

These bottle greens-ambers-browns,
transparent tints shattered
into crusted barrels, stains blistered to hands —
you know Virgil's been there all day.

Scissors

She appeared in my class with an oxygen tank
and a drive to make prints no matter what.
Culling savage images from Nat'l Geographic
battling her decline past the years of devoted sacrifice.

Her cut-out words, scorched and rehashed in quietude,
torn from fraudulent chronicles, the mouths
of sports figures twisted from games, war, city streets —
future genocides exacting revenge.

Her gnarled hands feathered the acid bath
biting the metal plates, to print figures running
from burning houses, arms waving, hair on fire.
She reveled in newspaper blood.

When I read the papers, I see my twin brother crawling
into pizza ovens to clean, failed into poverty.
He died in an old soldiers' home near Tacoma.
On the river today, the pile driver shoring up the old pier

with creosote beams, the dredger scooping up silt
with its long crane and basket-jaws — and her scissor's
nickel-plated steel, their weight in my hand,
their deep cutting edge.

Black Clock

Tumbling alphabets and numbers:
Cézanne's black clock without hands
near the crimson shell,
the sculpted white table cloth.

Geometry of the broken landscape
a divine order: *I am the primitive*
of the way I discovered —
bodies seen in space curve out, walls collapse.

The sequence of the spectrum
hatched in strokes
across the clear image,
his impossible fulcrum unfixed.

The black clock's pitchforks:
4:44 — the numbers speak
not our words, of
the threshold sentry.

The seed in the flux of sensations.
Palindrome time waiting between
the real & the unreal waking.
It's what is and back again.

The digital red colons flipping over
9:09 11:11 12:21 5:05 —
into numerical green sequences,
nor the pabulum of the crowd.

Without an observer nothing forms:
blood lust words all lies — actions rule
the growing galactic graveyard,
emptying the mind.

The music all around is all
to listen & listen,
the simultaneity of life
burned into the brushstrokes.

Reading the Flames

More murder & corruption & greed —
like the cheap plastic sink fittings
made in China that leak during breakfast,
re-reading the morning SF Chronicle.

What can we infer from newsprint?
Is the meaning of life the
evolution of consciousness —
to know — to be
to fit plumbing together …
pancakes & reading each other?

I washed the dishes clear of syrup.
Canadian geese flew out
swirling in a mass high up, calling out
to hook-up & flow in long lines — the echo
of their honking, fading quietly along the river.

In the short silence: an image I dreamt
last night of Oliveira's
ghost circus made of stained
washes & white smears — peopled with
calligraphy of the fine lined-blizzards.

This morning's fog, a soft harp of
Whistler's empty nocturnes blue-green-grey,
scraping the paint back to field — to
the back, to the white beginning.
The plates set out on checkered-blue cloth.

Thanks for the ginger pears (WCW might have said)
in the August refrigerator, they do
everything to escape our
pettiness, thought & ruin —
if I eat them now.

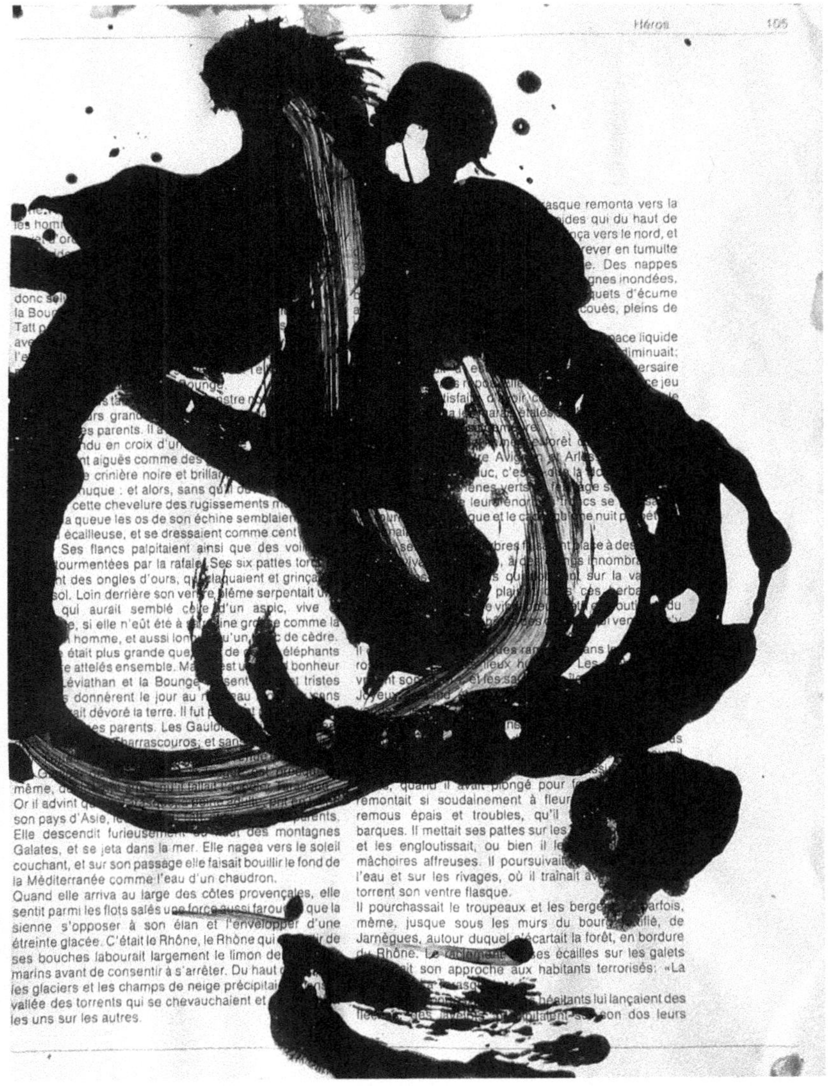

Elle descendit furieusement du haut des montagnes
Galates, et se jeta dans la mer. Elle nagea vers le soleil
couchant, et sur son passage elle faisait bouillir le fond de
la Méditerranée comme l'eau d'un chaudron.
Quand elle arriva au large des côtes provençales, elle
sentit parmi les flots salés une force aussi farouche que la
sienne s'opposer à son élan et l'envelopper d'une
étreinte glacée. C'était le Rhône, le Rhône qui ... ir de
ses bouches labourait largement le limon de...
marins avant de consentir à s'arrêter. Du haut ...

remontait si soudainement à fleur...
remous épais et troubles, qu'il ...
barques. Il mettait ses pattes sur les...
et les engloutissait, ou bien il le...
mâchoires affreuses. Il poursuivait...
l'eau et sur les rivages, où il traînait a...
torrent son ventre flasque.
Il pourchassait le troupeaux et les berge... parfois,
même, jusque sous les murs du bourg ...fié, de
Jarnègues, autour duquel s'écartait la forêt, en bordure
du Rhône. Le ... ses écailles sur les galets
...it son approche aux habitants terrorisés: «La

Honey

They turn and carry
by their breath
the wine of all winds

*Unfathomable mind
now beacon, now sea*
a spinning wheel

Filling wax with nectar
drowning in ritual acts
of light

The octagon of the newly
formed cell potion
the orchard keeper keeps

Twice-born
a lion's precise horde
empties the seed center

Minute in & minute out
the single pathway to the
transparent mountaintop

Then they gather the invisible
from a clearing
& all space wells up shouting.

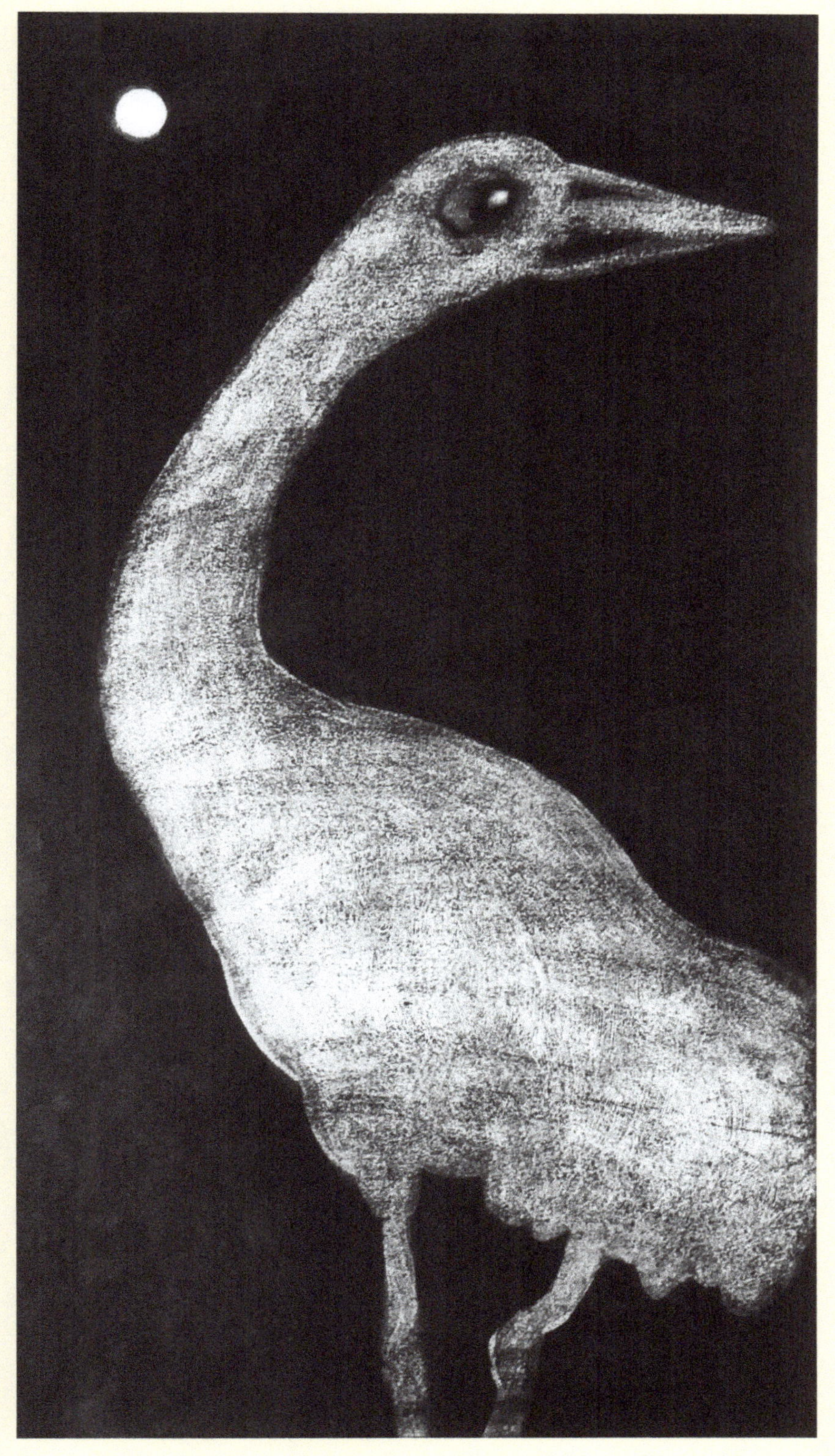

3

Flies of Les Baux

We drove into the Provence Valley
near Arles past its amphitheatre
and settled our rooms with the clerk.

Hungry for lamb chops their green boots
laughing at the wine steward, stern in
his black leather apron covering his ample

stomach and snarl: Grenache or Rosé blend?
(settled on full-bodied Merlot after arguments).
We finished with cheeses, apple slices, a walk

through the Mistral blowing off the Alps
in late summer, stars lit our way
under the blue night we grieved for.

In the morning we entered limestone caves
of Sarragan, with Egyptian guardian eyes carved
over entrances by Roman workers,

craggy quarries Dante wrote
his Purgatory from or that Van Gogh
painted his most Freudian image of —

led us from depths to heights,
the medieval village atop white rock,
a ruined château-fortress

rebuilt over centuries, cobbled streets
awash with tourist busloads —
the black buzz crossed our faces.

Hands swat back and forth, human
habitation started in 6000 BC, then
catapult wars, royalty disposed, regained.

Overlooking vineyards, olive groves, angled
plains of bonfires, seeds
clamoring to return a yellow radiance

waiting in us, surviving the scars
the nights strangled in secret rivers —
the black spots of flies humming for centuries.

A One Cent Magenta, 1856

We give and seek in return
in Latin bordering,
a scarlet octagon stamp with
sailing ship, black scribbles
to the left, smudges and
washes from handling.

The girl that collected stamps
lived at the Governor
General's Palace, a daughter
of the kitchen crew and her
aunt Victorie
scavenged for stamps in the
royal trash then
pasted them in a book — including
the world's rarest a One Cent
Magenta, date 1856.

It was a blue Sunday
on the island,
a storm had taken down
a row of tulip trees,
now there was a quiet
twittering in bushes,
the invisible dropping of

rainwater from leaf
to leaf — the mail schooner lay
anchored in a cove,
a white rowboat came ashore
with few letters.

She was watching the streaks
hinged then gliding
over the green expanse,
tropical trade winds
caught her skirt, a map drawn
with dashed lines.
Inland volcanic escarpments,
arched waterfalls
sheltering swifts flying
magnetically.
Two rare stamps lost: Toco
Toucan & Scarlet Macaw.

Noon, hidden in
dry stream beds narrowing
to the sea, she
rearranged forgotten
campfire stones
into shapes of spotted
quail and fuchsia flowers.

Magistrates in Victorian white suits
detecting watermarks
with chemical ethers —
Gothic script appearing
slowly then fading, the
minutiae of an engraved world —
Whorls ravenous, sea turtles,
emerald rain forests
searching for ancestors, jungle jaguars —
Conquerors,
sugar factories, sawmills, a
brewery in British Guiana.

The stamp grew in
a dark trunk
with daily commotion
surrounding it, became
the one spot of color left
stained in time, of
three-rigged masts, black
governing strokes signed
to cancel the collection, she
spent a childhood
running down the beach for …

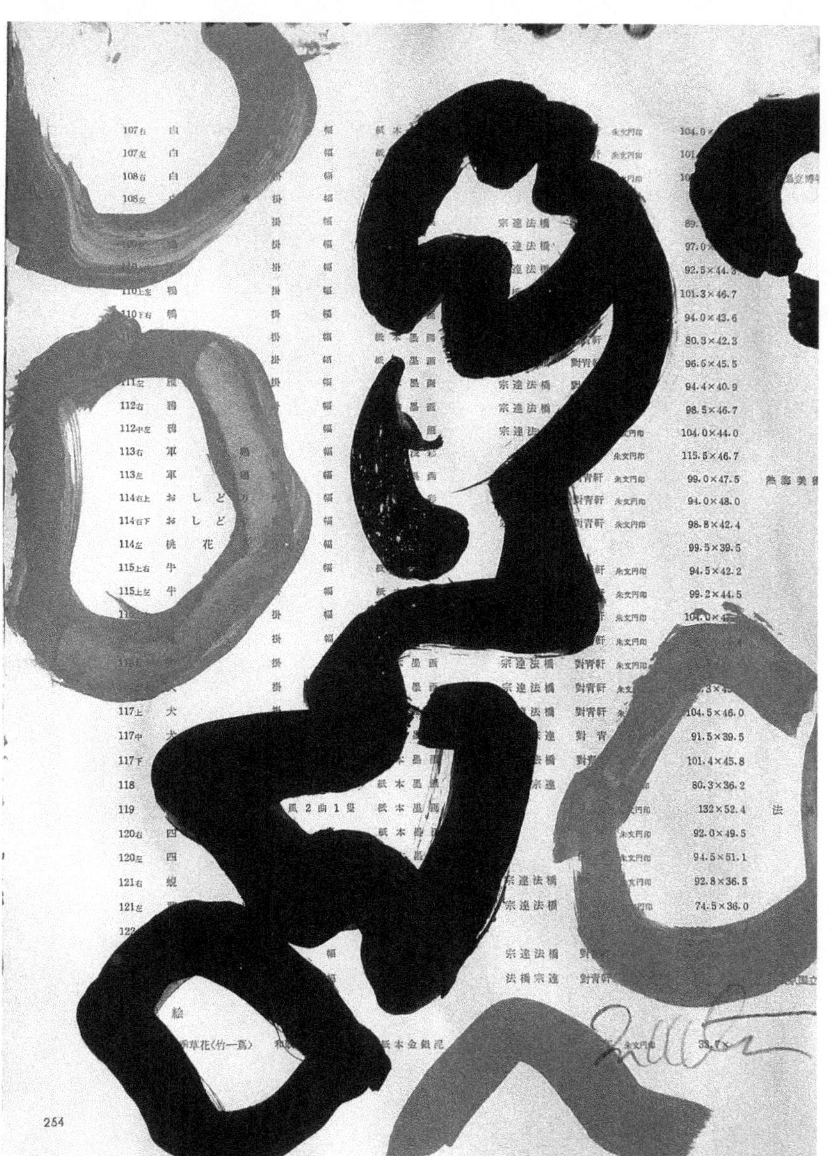

107右　白
107左　白
108右　白
108左
110上左　鴨
110下右　鴨
111左　鴨
112右　鴨
112中左　鴨
113右　軍
113左　軍
114右上　お　し　ど　り
114右下　お　し　ど
114左　桃　花
115上右　牛
115上左　牛
117上　犬
117中　犬
117下
118
119　紙2曲1隻
120右　四
120左　四
121右　娘
121左　娘
122
絵
草花〈竹一篇〉
宗達法橋
宗達法橋
宗達法橋
對青軒
朱文円印
紙本墨画
紙本金銀泥
89.
97.0×
92.5×44.3
101.3×46.7
94.0×43.6
80.3×42.3
96.5×45.5
94.4×40.9
98.5×46.7
104.0×44.0
115.5×46.7
99.0×47.5
94.0×48.0
98.8×42.4
99.5×39.5
94.5×42.2
99.2×44.5
104.0×
104.5×46.0
91.5×39.5
101.4×45.8
80.3×36.2
132×52.4
92.0×49.5
94.5×51.1
92.8×36.5
74.5×36.0
33.
熱海美術
法

Riding Horses at Kula San

She was a dark beauty, daughter to Director of the Sanitorium
on the island of Maui, at the 3000 foot level of the Haleakalā volcano.
We had gone swimming at Kihei and now we saddled her horses
for a ride around the red dirt roads bordering pineapple fields in Kula.

The brown horses were spirited and eager to leave the soft loam roads
for paths into the hills, they rushed to ends of a fence and waited
listening for some silent command from the volcano above, she gave them
the word *Mahkay* meaning death in Hawaiian.

Her black hair curled around her neck and flew up in gusts of wind,
intense eyes could not laugh because she knew all the stories
told about the Sanitorium built for consumptive
patients. Orange-pink Birds of Paradise grew along the roads.

In 1927 the TB deaths began, bacilli drifted in wet air,
caught hold deep in the lungs, until with coughing convulsions
they dropped in the green fields and were littered to Kula San,
immigrant Filipino, Portuguese, Spanish, Japanese.

As a child she saw St Elmo's Fire rolling down Sanitorium hallways,
violet-blue lightning balls like the sputum emptied into jars outside of doors,
a luminous plasma Pacific sailors saw during thunderstorms —
the hissing, buzzing sounds which glowed and led their way to the Islands.

Our horses' necks and haunches lathered and foamy
fell on Bougainvillea vines, long Pineapple leaves,
led us into small hills without paths, frenzied and caught up with the wind.
She didn't notice my gestures to stop, my lack of breath —

Only her eyes shone white from the history of night sweats
and weight loss, of those blue specters she forgot in feverish longing,
children's friends she saw come, then go down the long corridors,
who appeared hesitantly again, while riding horses in island wind.

24 Places

Seven orange-grey Flicker feathers
found at Los Trancos Creek — a scent of violet
in the silt a human gold tooth.

*

Green bottle of Framboise brandy
bought in Nice near the roman Amphitheatre
— whimsical Raspberry for after dinner dramas.

*

In a Yosemite autumn 3 Sun Dogs
orange smoky vapor in high Sierra skies
— glowing lights in a row of dense fog.

*

Mexican red circle collage on Baja street
a child made in school —
not the obvious, changing in spiral form.

*

Lake City pharmacy magazine rack,
Tanguy melting pocketbook covers, Dante's
drawing transfers — my secret gun powder elements.

*

Martinez cargo train's long whistle
across the Carquinez Strait in a summer evening
— seals barking in the brackish water.

*

White metal grid along the highway
to Vallejo, detached air duct covering
flung upside down — triangular.

*

Storage in the Arsenal: the Rokeby Venus,
rusted hoop hung on a nail, a perspective box —
her face across the Mirror on page 35.

Hobo blankets near Palo Alto train tracks,
emerald-throated pheasants under cardboard
— arch of orange peels on the wet earth.

*

Down the streets of Longview
passing whispers to sneaking cats
in night gutters — moon crescent cupping the sky.

*

San Mateo's *find the clue below the line*
shimmers inverted — a table set for
a blind man in a glass jar.

*

At Mac's Smoke Shop they talk
of Shades *the flashlight* Eddy —
mingling decay with the Sports Page.

*

In the Stanford eucalyptus grove
great horned owl feathers —
Hecate's hissing unguents.

*

With the masseuse on El Camino,
Lumi's long nipple a once buried rune
— the protruded root of Ancestors.

*

In the Port Angeles motel oval mirror
the wish-bone dance of her tilted pelvis —
tight slippery pouch reflected in the sound.

*

On Alpine Road pedaling the river rocks
in a knapsack down to Alma Ave —
the spiral carving in the hard flat rock.

Seattle swamps in the outer woods,
lavender veins in Fawn Lilies —
Yellow Adder's Tongue in the rain.

*

El Camino Real, wild mustard seeds
the Spaniards planted to return in spring
— spread to San Gregorio beach during summer.

*

Under the Radar Dish above Palo Alto
tan oak fungus pods in summer grasses —
red-tailed hawks & owls mounting the hills.

*

On Maui the lava rock, golden labia
of beehive along the dry stream bed —
brown Chukars trilling in thickets.

*

Island quail baths in soft dirt
under Mimosa branches on lava ledges —
cobwebs sheathed in golden light.

*

Up Haleakalā volcano the soft feathers
tucked into notebook leaves —
after digging with bird bones at the cave.

*

In the Mesquite the moth necklace
around the tree growing out of rock —
clumps of algae drifting into center pool.

*

Island chaparral House Finch among Kiawe thorns,
orange-red Cardinals in branches —
the spotted Dove cooing in the open road.

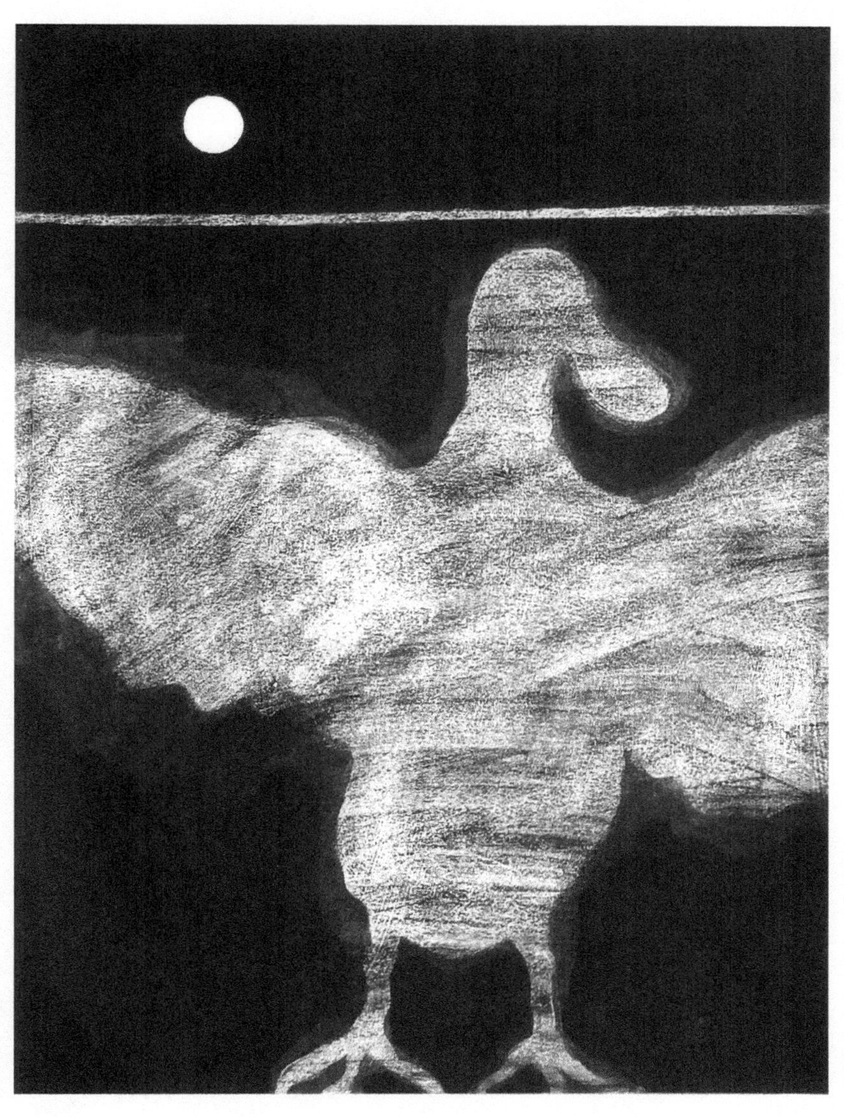

Night Opera, Santa Fe

From an open air desert proscenium
she appeared in theatre wings of dead souls
seeking rebirth on Jacob's Ladder —
Schoenberg at his most obtuse angle.

The green-blue light from below
caught her cheek bones her eyes
set in dark cavities haunting
her ragged sheath to dance.

Clashing voices colliding figures
rising again then diminishing
in that Bardo state between planes
moaning writhing upward.

Aurelia seasoned dancer taken
three depths below where painted labyrinth
scrims stretched over wooden bones
among stage props & scenery changes.

Fallen silences cultivating heart
coupled his stage hand to her opera spirit,
her labia glistening in darkness
sounds deep within her throat.

Arms thrashing released to heaven
sent her flickering motions up
into desert fires burning
on mesquite hills the real color

of hell beckoning her performance,
for added impact for visceral evidence
Schoenberg's atonal waver
straining for release into space.

Smeared facial paint, her red tights
rolled to ankles the costume tresses
flung up into cold stars going blind,
their idiot's song their hidden murmurings

coming through the other side of night.

Mont Saint-Michel, 1980

The four of us exhausted from driving
approached the mountain —
Jacques drove the blue Mercedes
all day, we were longing for a rest.

The island with a castle seen
from a great distance
belonged to the sea, returned at nightfall
a rocky tidal island in Normandy.

Benedictine abbey — medieval castle Sanctuary:
1300 years of history in the gulf of Saint-Malo,
on a flood plain the constant flow of
beggars, bell-ringers, ghosts, knights.

Gothic cloister arches, a prison in Napoleon's reign,
sea serpent views from the ramparts
crimson amoebas swirling in the rivers' silt
into the English Channel.

The island amidst & above the ending of time
— the Virgin Spring:
man's plague-ridden, sin-sickened, war-torn
existence, lest we become our tormentors.

A dialogue of conscience,
St. Michael as warrior,
trembling the dark to affirm the light,
the mountain an inverted cup

of spilled bile and wars
the invisible bees
built a golden hive upon,
the mountain became the wind.

Became nothing —
the free movement of gulls
that laid siege from long marches,
the mountain remained simply.

Beyond eyes burned out or chests
branded with hot irons,
the platform of light
the mountain in the sea.

The sea mixed with the sun,
the magnetic mountain
until limbs broke under the wheel —
spectral wanderers, pilgrims on

erratic roads, apparitions, the possessed
the haunted
emerged through gritted teeth,
the ravages and casualties

marched on across the wild waters
to contract the white airs
evaporated in convulsive echoes
at the outcropping in the sea.

Until the flame of the mountain
revealed itself, vertical wavering
light, hovering in the center —
the Ghost hunting for its own traces.

Treasure Island, SF

Brother Antoninus lay on the table,
the job interviewer's copy of his poems
I took as my own, the bait taken I passed
the test, my time to get a job in 1968.

San Francisco was in the heat
of Vietnam, domestic agonies peppered
the streets — the Feds were shipping
male virgins off to die and

Doctor Rigney of North Beach
had written to the draft board
about my *personality disorders*
& artistic bents for peace.

I took the Market Street trolley
to the Oakland bus terminal
for a ride out to the supply depot,
my first day on the job as shipping clerk.

Walking the hallways
looking for my appointed room
new soldiers stood in lines
waiting to be processed, then

Two called out my name —
the Frost brothers from Seattle
looking hopeful I was joining
them? *No, got a job here*

I hurried along … until my room,
there two heavy-set men
Daryl & Lenny stared back at me
under long rows of metal shelves.

Army parts to be shipped to Nam,
the guys showed me the ropes, then
we sat down for lunch, I read poetry
I told them, but not how I got the job.

I had the job they told me, but had
to attend their Baptist church on Sundays,
actually part of the job, or else.
I finished out the day, then headed home

Disappearing among the commuters
crowding buses into San Francisco,
as the sun went down the pacific fog
rolled in & I read my Brother Antoninus.

Posing for Los Alamos Housewives

I arrived late in my G-string
improvised from a plastic cord and cloth —
my first time posing for a drawing class.

I traded my modeling for a week's free drawing,
all I had to do was get to Los Alamos,
so Cherie picked me up and drove me there.

We went up the valley of the Rio Grande
talking about the etiquette of posing
for scientists' wives in a restricted enclave.

Cherie introduced me and I changed my clothes,
all the women twittering in the narrow room
around the edges of an elevated model stand

looked up as I entered, my cloth apparatus tied
around my hips for a pose of crossed arms
and twisted legs, as I started to shake and quiver

the ladies laughed until my wrap-around fell down.
They murmured softly, not that I was much to see,
anything that young and foolish was new to them,

who sat in living rooms waiting daily for husbands
to return from experimenting with new radiation,
with the bomb-to-be, a baby before the bath, the black rain

falling down upon Hiroshima, my skin burned and caked a
white ash, the red core gleaming through the cracks, the flesh
grease dropping onto the wooden floor, sparking

little fires, long streams of white smoke, hot crackles —
the ladies drew into their pages with charcoal and red
ink, smeared with the palms of their fists, into spit of their days.

The Window

What was I looking for in New Mexico that summer the heat
blurring strip malls from the Greyhound window all the way
to Santa Fe — my marriage gone, Eve's green eyes waking
ruinous-strange in San Francisco?

What led me later from job to job — opera stagehand,
waiter, construction worker, studio model — torn
across dusty adobe yards, street shadows stalking
the arrival of morning, aimless as myself?

What did I find by not looking, half-bound, half-asleep
in the mesquite and sage — an afterimage
of aspen gold in the Sangre de Cristos on a Tuesday
morning? What kept me painting

As if nothing had happened — I stretched opera canvas
4' x 5' over plywood: a lost pilgrim family
faceless in their long robes, a spider
catching a fish, a woman's mad smile turning to mist?

What caught me in between the burning
waters and the plateaus — in its sleep the city never sank,
its golden light a meal of desert music,
crested in a tree of the unexpected?

What phantasms in arroyos, poor bones left
in Eagle Nest near Taos — I leveled scaffolding for
a spiral chapel on a hill across from Angel Fire
until winter came, then hitched out across the desert

for San Francisco at New Year's Eve.

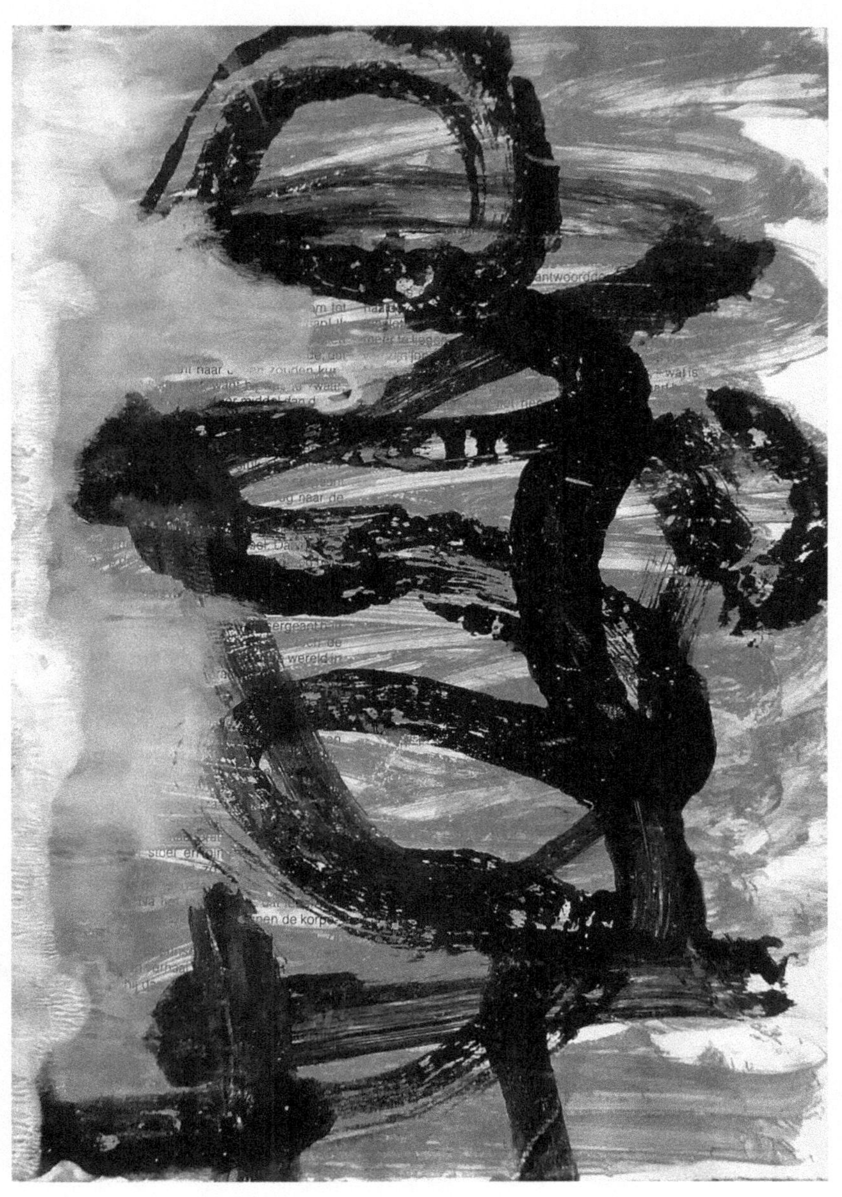

In Lusby

The clattering cicadas in trees,
the Luna Moth a red slab of meat
feasting on a light bulb.

In the first instance
one went against the grain,
not so in Lusby.

One was open & available,
the animals sought us out,
a rabbit sat calmly

staring as we drove in,
a deer stopped & looked
as we washed dishes,

a trap-door spider
lumbered among the leaves.
Black obsidian glass of

the Miocene sharks' teeth
found on a Chesapeake beach,
as the thought thickened

the computer box winked
its imperious gloat before
all was lost between the wires.

The first cause is not enough,
any reason for being
such as we are

driven inward by forces
on an awkward path,
stalking us.

Our Lady, Star of the Sea

Solomons, Maryland

Two paintings in the alcove room
from the chapel where
a soprano echoed through
the halls, held

his attention: a haloed fisherman's
fist around a net,
a smile on his face, back
with a full catch — next to him hung

a derelict boat sinking
into a brown moss-haze,
water overtaking its empty form —
the figure is the space.

Solitude in a room reversed
his conviction of all things rendered
because they are, utterances
scribbled in a notebook.

A child ran dancing into the room,
wide-eyed yelps in dark curls,
her father chasing after her
saw a silent man writing.

Years later will remember him
as a moment of peace
when it is needed, while
the writer holds the image

of the child as a vibrant sound
in his insulated moments.
Disturbed he left the room then
peered through the reflected

glass obscuring
everyone standing before
the ascending figure.
The minister slowly saw him,

his witnesses swaying
on either side, lifted-up on toes
with all hands joined together,
singing and singing.

After the service
the minister found the writer
back in the empty room,
peered in: *Is there anybody here?*

Saw him: *Oh …*
& left to greet his people
on their way home,
shaking their hands goodbye.

The Cave

Where are we going?
into the mouth of a cave
at Murphys in the Sierras
deep in gold country.

To pass through is enough,
down the long stairs
almost stumbling over our names,
the black closing round us.

What are we listening to?
the melted earth hanging in
slabs and dripping
ochre red sienna umber.

I can't explain it,
floors and walls flooded
out of time all battles
unfolded in downpours.

We return again to
the cataclysmic boredom
secreted away
beyond the dreaming trees.

Our traces the blind shadows
flickering on the cave walls,
we are not in the seed
of all things, not —

Roiling in the invisible sea
above the plain where
we first heard our bee hum,
the living waters turning.

There's something missing here,
the jeweled breath
when the cave was Mother
to flame-scattering bones.

Her lost deep-throated laugh
permeates the fixed strata,
our only feeling of rhythm
left by erasure or absence.

It doesn't matter any longer,
something dimly radiant
hovering near
the stone ceiling of night.

We no longer know when
the forest falls asleep or
when the animals
have their theatre.

Everything echoes now,
a day has passed,
we lie down and
face the sky.

Radio News

I'm always chopping old bread
just enough for the birds,
listening to the BBC.

The dusty wars and refugees,
a dry Gruyère olive-garlic loaf
in crumbs for the Spring Lake birds.

This morning I'm preparing —
people are rioting
against meltdowns crackups collapses.

My blind demented mother lives here,
a child newly discovering
the moon-lit garden & dancing.

On NPR Greek job & pension cuts,
Molotov cocktails over the meat
cleaver — a slight mold powders up

these golden crumbs zip-locked
now for the mallards
& red-winged blackbirds.

I lie down into the soft
lawn near the lake to scatter
word-crumbs round my body.

Robins & sparrows slowly arrive,
then a dozen or more
to eat and sing together.

My body is a table
on the earth,
the chopping block is scarred

from a knife spinning,
always waiting. Blue-green
ducks & black birds

dropping from umbrella
trees, chattering
and flying up again.

Unit K

She was the Ferndale daughter
of a farmer called Garlick, from English pioneers
near the Canadian border.

Reading the pages out of
order, the contour of her face, a rope that broke
into the debris of Unit K.

Screw all of you, I'm going to jump!
she yelled over the sports channel,
no one listening.

Still waiting in the courtyard,
electronic wrist cuff like a plastic
flea collar, indelible yellow

logo. *Am I a prisoner here?*
My shame at lying to her
to leave her, sitting there staring

into the absolute sky, a nearby
sparrow plucking out
a California poppy heart.

For a minute we sit in
full silence, turned away from
what bewilders us, an angel

without laughter or tears, clear shapes traced
from stones, and we look at each other,
her right hand pushes past her shocked

white hair, asks proudly *where is everybody?*
I can't find you, wherever that is …

Between the meadow lark
And the evening tide.

The Joke Table

At first, I thought it would be fun
to sit & listen at the Joke Table, the punch lines
well-chosen for the likes of us —

at the assisted-living they pay
and pay until they pass away
into the dark waters of Spring Lake.

Every first Sunday before breakfast
the Jokers summon those to roast
wise-cracking & crinkle-eyed.

We sit expecting to lighten our day
content to proceed without knowing
only that the food will arrive soon.

Around an ordinary table four decrepit men
white & angry, their past — pilots, reps, agents — hanging
from them like tumors.

Stuart, a Belgium paper salesman
his papers stacked before him, sermonizes in a 40's
radio voice sonorous and glib,

his Internet jokes about race
drugs poverty sex —
old rancor from his silent days.

He & his immigrant parents scrounging
through the Depression for wood for rent,
the humiliation of being unread.

By then, I was fatigued in my chair, or
until egg breakfast plates put before us,
the ice-rattle against the water glass —

I felt the space around the table,
our ad hoc choices pulsing red cells sweating.
Thank you very much

said my finely-tuned cerebrum
in my softest voice,
as I rose to leave without a smile.

Eyes of the Sorcerer

Having left Seattle and visited relatives in San Francisco
the Newlyweds
headed for Mexico in the late summer,
with camping gear
and a tent strapped to the roof of their car
they crossed the border
and sped
into the desert between small towns.
The first day
a station wagon passed them loaded with several families
on their way
to Rosario and hit head-on an oncoming car.

The two cars spun in opposite directions and came to a stop
far from the road.
The Newlyweds pulled over and rushed to the dying on front seats,
the dazed
wandering into the desert, the children crying and luggage strewn
in spirals.
Covered in blood from comforting them, they left when a farm truck
arrived to carry away
the dead and dying, up the road they washed in a gas station
and drank some beer
to keep their bile down. Later they camped in their tent

along the ocean,
in the night packs of wild dogs roamed around and
barked in the wind.
Tortoise and conch shells were found in the morning along edges
of the beach.
They ate some fruit they had brought with them and walked in the sun
under long lines of pelicans.
In Mazatlán they found an apartment with a balcony and settled in
for a week.
The Dia de los Muertos festival carried them downtown with candy
skulls, fireworks
and costumed skeleton crowds, later sleeping in their beds
a large dark bird flew in
through the curtains and out again.

In the morning shopping for oranges they passed a barber shop
and a man pointing
to a newspaper where his favorite dead face stood out from a grid of
dead faces on the front page,
collected from a bus accident in the jungles south of town.
Several
days later they drove south to a little town on the sea.
Mayan ruins on the hills, overgrown
damp vines hung onto the road, in the town a candle shop
and astrology reading table
run by
a young couple from the States were empty.

They found a cement apartment on the beach
where green lizards crawled
along the walls. As they moved their camping equipment and
luggage into their room,
they were invited to dinner by a local Brujo who introduced
himself to them
at the foot of the stairs.
Later that evening they went to the address given by the Brujo,
inside were human skulls
and candles burning, animal fetuses in amber jars, parrot and eagle feathers,
with leopard skins
and black rocks in leather straps hanging from the ceiling.
He greeted them
and they sat down around a table.

What they ate placed them immediately in a cage as two black birds.
To keep the Brujo awake
they sang for him and he rewarded them with golden seeds and sweet water.
They never returned
to Seattle or San Francisco again.
On their cage were the words *Ojos de Brujo*.

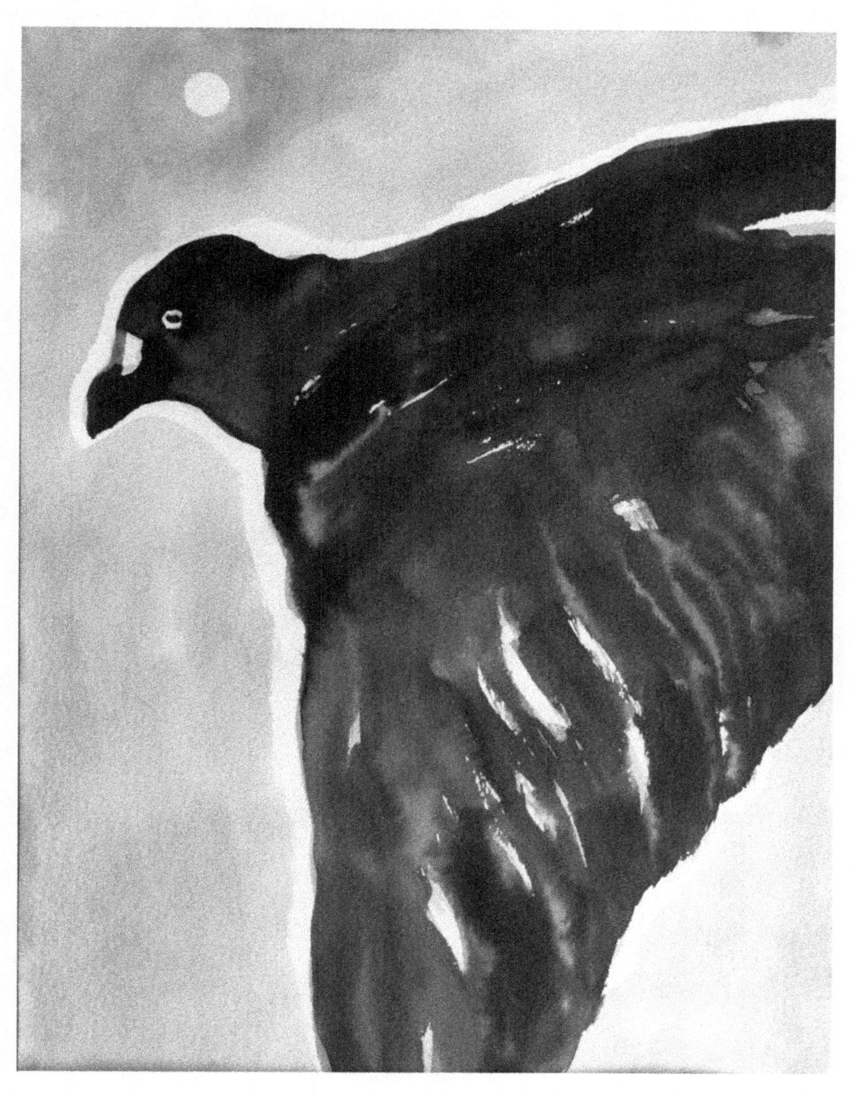

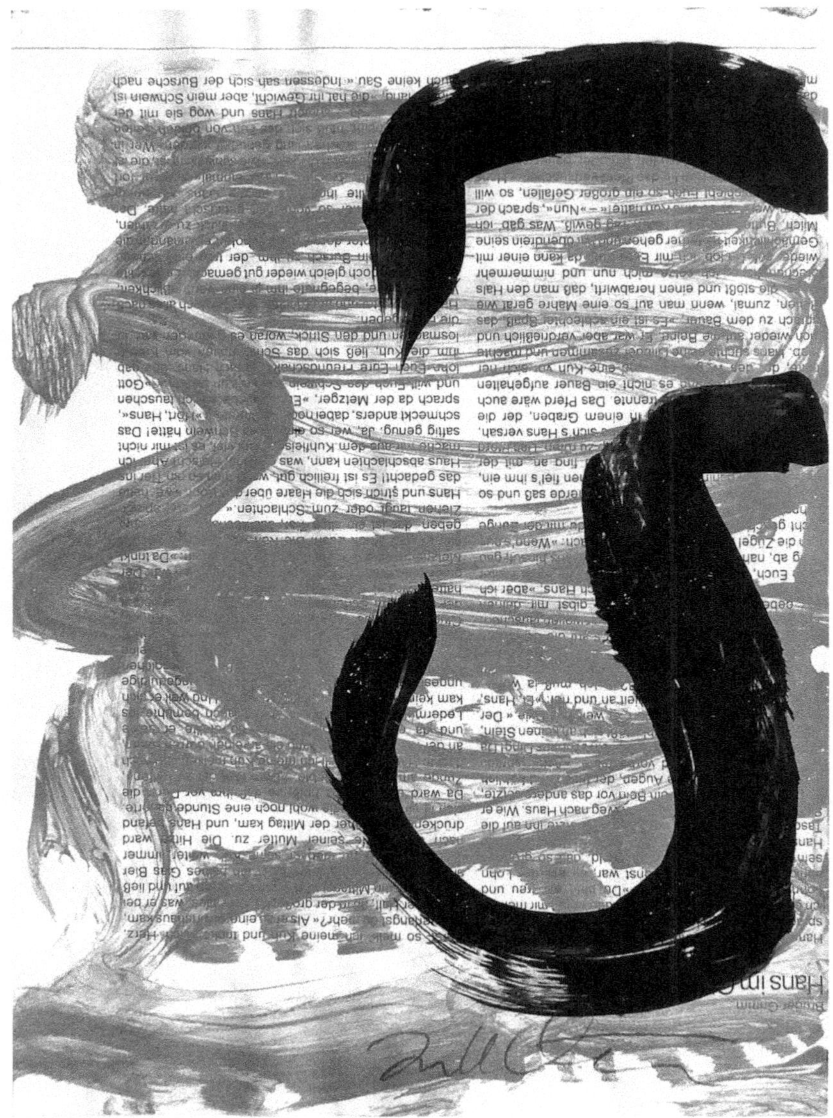

Haircut in Deauville, 1980

Ferme Saint Siméon

We drove out to Deauville for my haircut,
two giant grey geese flew in front of our car.
It was late Autumn and the boardwalk was empty
of its film stars, striped cabanas, topless beauties —
scoundrels in white suits lurked about the lobby,

potted palms and ceiling fans and parquet floors.
The ocean smell hung over the large room, its light
had faded the prints even in recessed hallways.
My hair stylist was young, red haired with brown eyes,
she wore a light green gown which opened in the front

and there much to my surprise her rose tipped breasts
fully prominent — I looked around the room and all the women
were topless save for their gowns: *Angelique, Bluet, Galice, Fuschia,
Mouron rouge, Narcisse des poètes, Clandestine, Lilas blanc,
Hortensia, Hyacinthe sauvage, Immortelle, Jasmin de Virginie.*

Flowering softness promising promising
all blossoms loosened tongues tempted incandescent roses
swelling gathered up wrinkled to a point of blood
purple flowers strange music wanting or desire.
We returned to Honfleur, birthplace of Baudelaire and Satie,

our residence a large farmhouse in the woods
below a children's school on the cliff overlooking the Harbor.
For dinner Mussels and Chicken in cream sauce, local Rosé wine,
desserts with aged apple brandy Calvados — my room was named Courbet
overlooking orchards, with a close view of ships passing into Honfleur.

Studio Door

A weathered metal door, of marine corrosion
and artist scratches, open to the rain.

Inside, many colored magnetic letters
visitors arrange, listing cryptic messages.

Outside, to the right, a jade tree
the sparrows chase each other around.

Front yard: import cars, the container and oil ships
eased-in by tugs, ocean cloisters at dock.

About this door: we pass through
in a hurry, or stroll out onto the porch, and sit.

An echo answers every echo,
until silence can restore us to a studio door.

We Live Here

by the river
in the Arsenal looking past
the cars from Japan,

the strait and the hills
in California light, breezes
from the Bay, where everything has stopped

for the holidays, but we are studio-busy
with coffee, paint, fresh tarts,
a productive day —

not much in the Book Review,
except last week 13 sparrows (all at once!)
flew into the studio and stayed an hour

flying around making noise
and I'm talking to them,
paintbrush in hand.

Benicia Laundromat

Yet it is not by their clothes
I know them — their eyes tell more, averted, downcast —
the scent-stains of fear, shit or age creased
in the underwear, the curious end-spaces
when the machine cycles finish.

They carry
bags and armfuls of soiled clothes
to this hum-sloshing strip-mall
and study them facing
the soapy fire, circular whirl

turning at once into each other, with
breathing masks or measured paces —
others, varicose thumbing of magazines,
pondering silent lists.

The lights' glare on white enamel,
the plastic yellow bubble on the black
clock ticking its red second hand, and
in the same sweep, the white lint bits
shaking out onto tile floors.

Hunting Feathers

Wild turkeys foraging in the fennel
groves at Lake Herman —

white-striped feathers
caught in the eucalyptus bark,

their bronze-tipped luster
black against speckled brown.

A row of giant trees & hooded notches
roosted-in, leaving speckled poop

over the waxy leaves, white circular spatters,
trampled stretches by turkey bands —

18 pecking at the seeded earth
the reversed sign of 7

scratched–on-the-elbow
from a fall downhill searching

for a turkey feather.

Landscape with Owls

The ghosts of sighs linger
from either side of the divide,
from the deep

fugue nested in an oak, from
a grove of owls. Or at noon,
on a hill crest the grey

fox runs to its burrow under
the freeway and back again.
Another way of speaking to

boundaries.
We know the distances:
just passing through, we say —

swell to be here while it lasts,
though can't prove what we see
except in artifice, except the golden

cage, helping itself to everything
we know. The crows pick at cow
bones in the summer

gulch, covering the evidence.
Our odd and dense
resonance collides with the day,

the friction sleeping in rock,
dreaming in plant, waking in sky,
and our perishing bodies inside

this fool's errand, this trial
by farce, frozen crackling
— everything is alive, first

as nuance then as ghostly thing,
insistent on being left unsaid.
The ghosts of sighs linger, I said.

The owl's sound pierces, wind
across the lake, white caps
spun by starlings.

Afternoons at Annecy, 1980

Twain and Cézanne visited in 1890s this four-story
four-star ivy-clad eleventh-century Benedictine stone abbey,
Hotel Abbaye de Talloires.
Twain's travel letters rescuing his Connecticut castle,
Cézanne's turbulence sneering at the picturesque in paint.

Twain, chronicler of vanities, hypocrisies, murders unmourned
common speech of the day —
found Lake Annecy under the music of soft gloom,
a brooding mystery in afternoons.
Like the Prince & Pauper who switch places, Twain predicted

he would go out with Halley's Comet return, born as two
unaccountable freaks, the sky reaching beyond darkness,
his humor slyly stamped
in black/white over yellow newspapers of New York,
now in two fathoms of safe water.

Cézanne, shy day-dreamer battling
for complete surrender to his *petite sensations*
outside the polite Paris hubbub,
focused his moment beyond identity at Mont Sainte-Victoire;
while in Annecy, he questioned the landscape

enveloping in atmosphere, structured a T on its side,
symmetries shattered
by the storm inside him,
diagonal strokes across the violet lake shadows
stormy bolts, energized shards — blue green black.

As for us, we arrived at Annecy in the late afternoon,
dined in the main room, a huge crackling fire,
tapestries, candle-lit alcoves, dinner of
cheese-tomato soup, fish quiche, lamb, wine.
Later in lounges along the Lake, cognac and smoking,

a shudder of early autumn under the wooden docks,
night swans eating trout fingerlings,
mist over the lake, sun rising
over the mountains & bird call —
by afternoon sailboats, hang gliders & water-skiers.

The Mississippian Twain, his swarthy roots in new land
touring Europe's châteaux
stocked with travel sketches,
back-pedaled the afternoons, smoking cigars
in white linen suits and panama hats.

Cézanne's sky shattered into diamond shapes, watery planes,
a brook rushing down
from the mountains
into the lake below, landscape of inner struggles
of wild forces ordered, round a relic of Middle Ages.

On the drive out of the Talloires
along the mountain roads we narrowly missed a fox,
a red-orange flash
above the blue lakes, a last glimpse
of gardens of grace — then disappeared

into the maple woods, a sound of bells
ringing every so often from hidden towers.

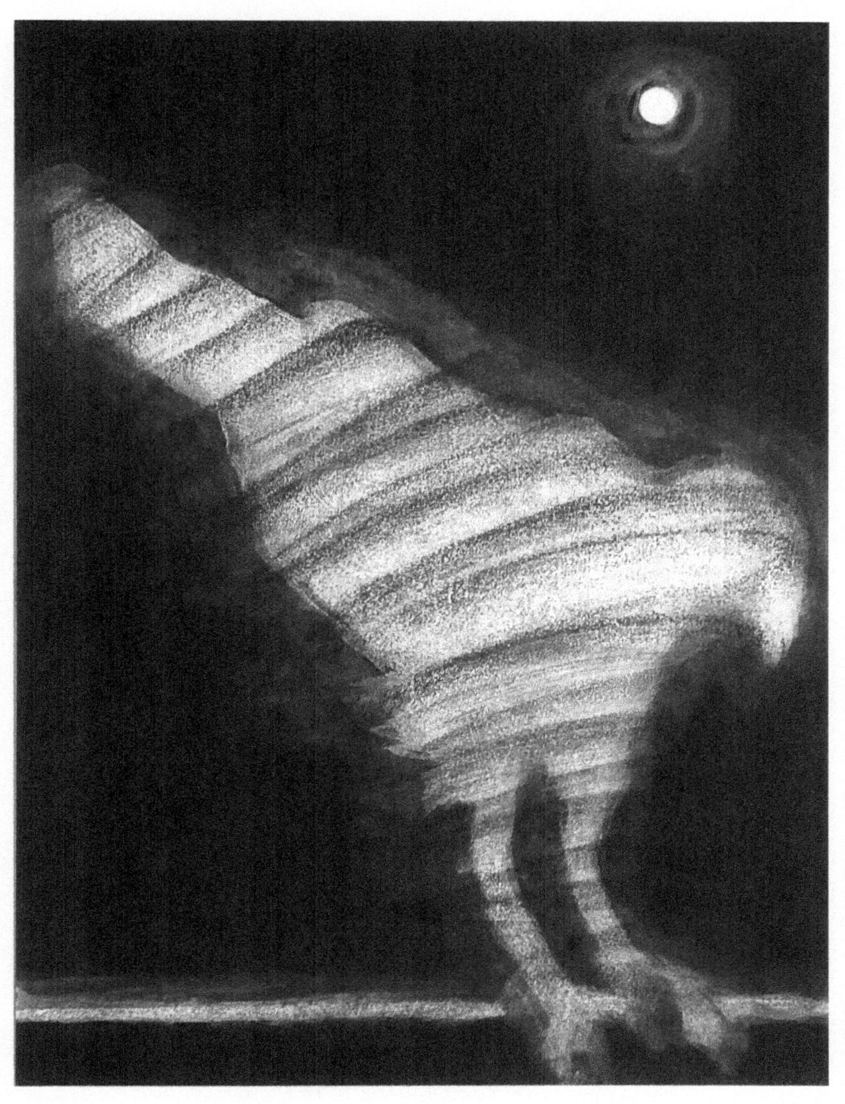

Climbing Mt. Haleakalā

She left the ocean shores, headed up the mountain
toward the volcano Haleakalā on the island of Maui.

Far from the road, in subdivisions excavators found
shaman bundles of bone and small stones, reburied them.

She walked into thorny Kiawe mesquite, startled
Chukar partridges, picked up a bamboo walking stick

in advance of walking, to catch silver lattice
spiders had woven over the sun.

She dislodged feathers caught in roots ruptured from rain.
Up parched arroyos Mimosa blew into pools of lava rock.

Ecstatic trilling, purple dragonflies, wild mint nettles.
Swirling sparrows crisscrossed small streams — the no-events

that happened for no one, perpetual states watched by
Turtle eye and Quail horns.

Into shadowed palms a cool quiet pervaded her steps,
a white moth curved near her head

disappearing into serpentine branches of Banyan trees,
golden Gecko lizards darted up the trunks and waited.

Wind caught the top hollow of her bamboo stave,
nearing volcanic caves piled with rocks, burials of forgotten tribes.

White Haole Forbidden Entry!
She smoothed out all traces in the soft red dirt,

bird tracks remained.
She passed the rock face, a large pool fed

by an unknown source, algae covered one part of the water.
Slipping in without clothes,

dark specks of leaves colliding in combustion
covered her feet, spiraled up round her legs —

then stepped out, singular
in a shaft of light.

She stretched, breathing heavily, listening
to the wind from the ocean below,

then walked on, up the mountain, taking down branches
with her bamboo,

one hand held out opening, the tree and the bird
speaking.

Wind pushed her fibers, her legs no longer moved,
the paper and the ink dissolved.

Light placed a star-cupped petal into her spiral pubis, what
song drew out of the whole space —

whispers passed to the wet earth, a white dust blooming out
of the stones on Maui.

Carquinez Strait

The waters begin slowly, rain falling into the mist,
under a full moon, the cool light we have inside of us

like seawater and calcium, night crawling along the dreaming
river bottom. The river lifting as air, until the Bay tides merge

where the two rivers, Sacramento and San Joaquin meet.
Seals bark in the brackish edges, skeletons at a feast, the eyes

of a man furious with fever, slip by, hieroglyphs pulled up
from the sand, then drifting down again into the remains.

Along the embankments graffiti trains, cargo ships like the
Andromeda Leader spilling bilge from stammering oceans,

a home among strangers. The river dredged over and over,
by the great net trembling time, a line inside a circle,

a skull inside a skin. Black tugs like *Orion II* pushing
ocean barges, the river all breath, bones, and eyes, indwelling

space of invisible salt, leaving our bodies, closing our eyes,
the waves pulling us along, almost to nothing —

the last word, not a word any longer, a borderless world
flaming out, *thaw and resolves itself into a dew* — the dust

of exploded stars, the birds of the hills, a movement toward
something else, the river formed by the bruises of our exchanges.

No time to rest voices, like tree limbs fallen after a storm, struck
by stupor, ripped through in a torrent. The river uncanny, dark

poisonous, seems to go on forever, yet we know it cannot.
All that we fear, we have exiled. Everything hidden germinates,

the smell of spleen, the deep undertow of orphaned states,
the pounds of flesh and the buckets of slime, a shrug of shoulders

the same as a sudden surge of wind across expanses. The darker
the waters the deeper the currents, the detour places that have no

connections, can't answer questions, the ovens still smoldering
somewhere. *We were away thinking about things.* The moon hanging

like a piece of skin, the river dies drooling like all of us, *the ocean
refuses no river.* The river's body falls-in suddenly, evaporates

and hurries away, the whole movement a faint smile, and beneath
so many screams, nothing rests, for what is pulled out of the waters —

we had jumped feet first into the fires. The river shapeless until it
reaches the banks, our eyes in the heat make noises in our throats,

a cadence of bird echoes, the deep green below, the white crests above.
The circulation is all, a kind of delirium, waking voices in the blood.

We are the thing we mock to be, the white flames over the red theatre,
the river light, its gold-powdered-reds, the wind has yet to extinguish.

A river of flotsam, solemnly estranged from scrap sources, in every
breath, in every cup of water, *it is and it isn't* until one goodbye isn't enough.

All evidence dispersed beyond the Milky Way, *if anybody calls tell them
we have gone* into the final river, of the music made of air.

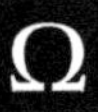

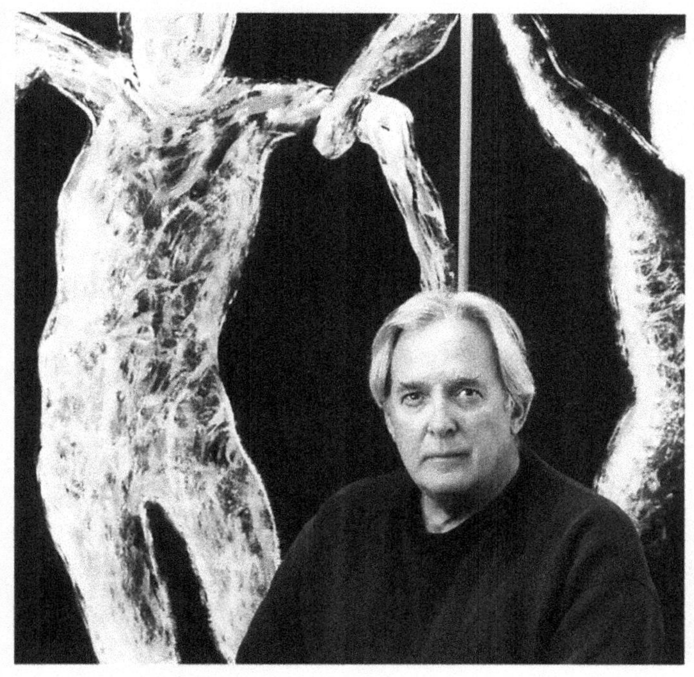

Lee Michael Altman studied poetry in the Pacific Northwest in the 1960s with Elizabeth Bishop and Galway Kinnell. He coedited a small literary journal Salted Feathers *which published such poets as Bukowski and Ginsberg. In the 1970s he received a BFA in Fine Arts from the University of Washington in Seattle. He continued his studies at Stanford with Nathan Oliveira and Frank Lobdell, receiving an MFA and teaching there after graduation. More of his timeline and activities can be viewed at* **www.paintsong.com** *which he shares with his wife, the painter Linda Grebmeier.*